MORNING SONG

MORNING SONG

Poems for New Parents

Edited by Susan Todd and
Carol Purington

St. Martin's Press
New York

www.stmartins.com

Design by Kathryn Parise

LIBRARY OF CONGRESS CATALOGING-IN-PUBLICATION DATA

Morning song : poems for new parents / [edited by] Susan Todd and Carol Purington.—1st ed.
    p. cm
    ISBN 978-0-312-64426-0
    1. Parent and child—Poetry.   2. Newborn infants—Poetry.
3. Parenting—Poetry.   I. Todd, Susan, 1941–   II. Purington, Carol.
PN6110.P25M67 2011
808.81'93525—dc22

                                                            2011007418

First Edition: May 2011

10   9   8   7   6   5   4   3   2   1

For our parents,
Barbara and Herbert Purington
Elma and Theodore Bagg, in memory

CONTENTS

II. Conception and Grace

III. Waiting

IV. Birth Day

V. Newest Child

VI. Sleep and Song

VII. At Play

VIII. Green and Carefree

IX. Lessons

X. Wisdom and Courage

XI. Of Night and Light and Half-Light

XII. Imagination and Memory

XIII. To Arrive Where We Started

That love is all there is,
Is all we know of love. . . .

—EMILY DICKINSON

MORNING
SONG

INTRODUCTION

This book began in friendship, and the friendship began in poetry. For more than fifteen years we have met every two or three weeks to read poems aloud with one another. We might give an afternoon or several months to one poet or to a theme or a season. Over time our explorations have led us to discoveries and connections and to a heightened sense of the power of poetry. With the prospect of a first grandchild it was natural then to assemble a collection of poems to celebrate that birth.

The original *Morning Song* was presented in a hand-made edition to the new mother and from the start the gift brought real pleasure to the family, becoming a well-worn possession admired by friends, other parents, and grandparents. Eventually we decided to add more poems to the volume—to embrace a wide audience that would include anyone anticipating a child—whether by birth or by adoption. Thus, this book . . .

Many anthologies are meant to introduce poetry to children; *Morning Song* is for parents. There are certainly poems in this book that will appeal to young listeners, but most of our choices are intended to honor and engage and speak to the inner life of mothers and fathers. This book recognizes that a child's progression toward maturity is inextricably bound to a parent's own lifelong journey.

We encountered numerous surprises in gathering these poems. Only a few have ever appeared together and many were tucked away in the nooks and crannies of literature—little-known poems by well-known authors. And for all the wisdom available for those having children, one essential thread had been left out—the thread that only poetry can provide. It is by the distilled and intimate language of the heart that we are truly invited to share and contemplate human experience. With the responsibility of opening every aspect of the world for a child, parents can take comfort in the knowledge that they are understood, that they are not alone, and that among their most enduring resources is poetry.

With sources ranging from the Bible to our contemporary culture, this anthology includes the cosmic and the comic, the spiritual and the pragmatic. It begins with poetry that touches on the elemental stirrings of all creation and expands to the place a child will one day have on the world's stage. Lyrical poems about romance and desire, exuberance and laughter are in dialogue with everyday poems about crying and nighttime feedings. Many express the essential role of nature in shaping the soul. Others shed light on those unpredictable times that lodge in a child's memory. There are poems about ideals and humor and about what you wish for your boy or girl—manners and courage, perseverance and a sense of adventure—and so many other weighty (and ephemeral) ideas that may get lost in the crowded days of parenthood.

Fortunately, there is always time to read a poem. Our hope is that *Morning Song* will become a treasured companion for all the hours and moods of waiting and caring for a child over many years, but most especially during the wonder-filled momentous beginning—the welcoming of a new life.

I

Beginnings

In your hearts are the birds and the sunshine

—"Children,"
Henry Wadsworth Longfellow

A Prayer in Spring

Oh, give us pleasure in the flowers today;
And give us not to think so far away
As the uncertain harvest; keep us here
All simply in the springing of the year.

Oh, give us pleasure in the orchard white,
Like nothing else by day, like ghosts by night;
And make us happy in the happy bees,
The swarm dilating round the perfect trees.

And make us happy in the darting bird
That suddenly above the bees is heard,
The meteor that thrusts in with needle bill,
And off a blossom in mid-air stands still.

For this is love and nothing else is love,
The which it is reserved for God above
To sanctify to what far ends He will,
But which it only needs that we fulfill.

Robert Frost

The Lamb

　　　　Little Lamb, who made thee?
　　　　Dost thou know who made thee?
Gave thee life, and bid thee feed,
By the stream and o'er the mead;
Gave thee clothing of delight,
Softest clothing, woolly, bright;
Gave thee such a tender voice,
Making all the vales rejoice?
　　　　Little Lamb, who made thee?
　　　　Dost thou know who made thee?

　　　　Little Lamb, I'll tell thee,
　　　　Little Lamb, I'll tell thee:
He is callèd by thy name,
For He calls Himself a Lamb.
He is meek, and He is mild;
He became a little child.
I a child, and thou a Lamb,
We are callèd by His name.
　　　　Little Lamb, God bless thee!
　　　　Little Lamb, God bless thee!

　　　　　　　　William Blake

The Creation

And God stepped out on space,
And he looked around and said:
I'm lonely—
I'll make me a world.

And far as the eye of God could see
Darkness covered everything,
Blacker than a hundred midnights
Down in a cypress swamp.

Then God smiled,
And the light broke,
And the darkness rolled up on one side,
And the light stood shining on the other,
And God said: That's good!

Then God reached out and took the light in his hands,
And God rolled the light around in his hands
Until he made the sun;
And he set that sun a-blazing in the heavens.
And the light that was left from making the sun
God gathered it up in a shining ball
And flung it against the darkness,
Spangling the night with the moon and stars.
Then down between the darkness and the light
He hurled the world;
And God said: That's good!

Then God himself stepped down—
And the sun was on his right hand,
And the moon was on his left;

The stars were clustered about his head,
And the earth was under his feet.
And God walked, and where he trod
His footsteps hollowed the valleys out
And bulged the mountains up.

Then he stopped and looked and saw
That the earth was hot and barren.
So God stepped over to the edge of the world
And he spat out the seven seas—
He batted his eyes, and the lightnings flashed—
He clapped his hands, and the thunders rolled—
And the waters above the earth came down,
The cooling waters came down.

Then the green grass sprouted,
And the little red flowers blossomed,
The pine tree pointed his finger to the sky,
And the oak spread out his arms,
The lakes cuddled down in the hollows of the ground,
And the rivers ran down to the sea;
And God smiled again,
And the rainbow appeared,
And curled itself around his shoulder.

Then God raised his arm and he waved his hand
Over the sea and over the land,
And he said: Bring forth! Bring forth!
And quicker than God could drop his hand,
Fishes and fowls
And beasts and birds
Swam the rivers and the seas,

Roamed the forests and the woods,
And split the air with their wings.
And God said: That's good!

Then God walked around,
And God looked around
On all that he had made.
He looked at his sun,
And he looked at his moon,
And he looked at his little stars;
He looked on his world
With all its living things,
And God said: I'm lonely still.

Then God sat down—
On the side of a hill where he could think;
By a deep, wide river he sat down;
With his head in his hands,
God thought and thought,
Till he thought: I'll make me a man!

Up from the bed of the river
God scooped the clay;
And by the bank of the river
He kneeled him down;
And there the great God Almighty
Who lit the sun and fixed it in the sky,
Who flung the stars to the most far corner of the night,
Who rounded the earth in the middle of his hand;
This Great God,
Like a mammy bending over her baby,
Kneeled down in the dust

Toiling over a lump of clay
Till he shaped it in his own image;

Then into it he blew the breath of life,
And man became a living soul.
Amen. Amen.

James Weldon Johnson

Children

Come to me, O ye children!
For I hear you at your play,
And the questions that perplexed me
Have vanished quite away.

Ye open the eastern windows,
That look towards the sun,
Where thoughts are singing swallows
And the brooks of morning run.

In your hearts are the birds and the sunshine,
In your thoughts the brooklet's flow,
But in mine is the wind of Autumn
And the first fall of the snow.

Ah! what would the world be to us
If the children were no more?
We should dread the desert behind us
Worse than the dark before.

What the leaves are to the forest,
With light and air for food,
Ere their sweet and tender juices
Have been hardened into wood,—

That to the world are children;
Through them it feels the glow
Of a brighter and sunnier climate
Than reaches the trunks below.

Come to me, O ye children!
And whisper in my ear
What the birds and the winds are singing
In your sunny atmosphere.

For what are all our contrivings,
And the wisdom of our books,
When compared with your caresses,
And the gladness of your looks?

Ye are better than all the ballads
That ever were sung or said;
For ye are living poems,
And all the rest are dead.

Henry Wadsworth Longfellow

April 5, 1974

The air was soft, the ground still cold.
In the dull pasture where I strolled
Was something I could not believe.
Dead grass appeared to slide and heave,
Though still too frozen-flat to stir,
And rocks to twitch, and all to blur.
What was this rippling of the land?
Was matter getting out of hand
And making free with natural law?
I stopped and blinked, and then I saw
A fact as eerie as a dream.
There was a subtle flood of steam
Moving upon the face of things.
It came from standing pools and springs
And what of snow was still around;
It came of winter's giving ground
So that the freeze was coming out,
As when a set mind, blessed by doubt,
Relaxes into mother-wit.
Flowers, I said, will come of it.

Richard Wilbur

Wheel

You on a tricycle the day I was born
    Brooklyn streets echoing your pedals
when the wheel of my lifetimes
    let me off in that hospital as
the sun glanced off Boston Harbor
    and you looked up then
to see it rise over a white frame house
    knowing that every once
in a while something shifts or
    the wheel clicks at certain events
then turns before the pause is noticed
    but for me and for you this was a time
when the earth called out and trees
    on the land here caught an April wind
the old farm felt a tremor
    and even the irises by the door
sensed they would someday be moved
    so for long Aprils to come
they would always remember
    in June they must bloom for you

                    Susie Patlove

The Song of Solomon

(excerpt)

The voice of my beloved! Behold, he cometh leaping upon the
mountains, skipping upon the hills.

My beloved is like a roe or a young hart: behold, he standeth behind
our wall, he looketh forth at the windows, shewing himself
through the lattice.

My beloved spake, and said unto me, Rise up, my love, my fair one,
and come away.

For, lo, the winter is past, the rain is over and gone;

The flowers appear on the earth; the time of the singing of birds is
come, and the voice of the turtle is heard in our land;

The fig tree putteth forth her green figs, and the vines with the tender
grape give a good smell. Arise, my love, my fair one, and come
away.

Song of Solomon, 2: 8–13
The Bible, King James Version

A Blessing for Wedding

Today when persimmons ripen
Today when fox-kits come out of their den into snow
Today when the spotted egg releases its wren song
Today when the maple sets down its red leaves
Today when windows keep their promise to open
Today when fire keeps its promise to warm
Today when someone you love has died
    or someone you never met has died
Today when someone you love has been born
    or someone you will not meet has been born
Today when rain leaps to the waiting of roots in their dryness
Today when starlight bends to the roofs of the hungry and tired
Today when someone sits long inside his last sorrow
Today when someone steps into the heat of her first embrace
Today, let this light bless you
With these friends let it bless you
With snow-scent and lavender bless you
Let the vow of this day keep itself wildly and wholly
Spoken and silent, surprise you inside your ears
Sleeping and waking, unfold itself inside your eyes
Let its fierceness and tenderness hold you
Let its vastness be undisguised in all your days

Jane Hirshfield

Wild Nights—Wild Nights!

Wild Nights—Wild Nights!
Were I with thee
Wild Nights should be
Our luxury!

Futile—the Winds
To a Heart in port—
Done with the Compass—
Done with the Chart!

Rowing in Eden—
Ah, the Sea!
Might I moor—Tonight—
In Thee!

Emily Dickinson

Sonnet 17

Who will believe my verse in time to come,
If it were fill'd with your most high deserts?
Though yet, heaven knows, it is but as a tomb
Which hides your life and shows not half your parts.
If I could write the beauty of your eyes,
And in fresh numbers number all your graces,
The age to come would say "This poet lies;
Such heavenly touches ne'er touch'd earthly faces."
So should my papers, yellow'd with their age,
Be scorn'd, like old men of less truth than tongue;
And your true rights be term'd a poet's rage,
And stretched meter of an antique song:
    But were some child of yours alive that time,
    You should live twice—in it, and in my rhyme.

William Shakespeare

II
Conception and Grace

the part of her
that's now child

—"Cello Suite,"
Robert Bagg

What Is the Beginning?

What is the beginning? Love. What the course? Love still.
What the goal? The goal is Love on the happy hill.
Is there nothing then but Love, search we sky or earth?
There is nothing out of Love hath perpetual worth:
All things flag but only Love, all things fail or flee;
There is nothing left but Love worthy you and me.

Christina Rossetti

Wanting to Have a Child

"Wanting to have a child," she said, "is like wanting
to make a garden." It was beginning
to be spring then, snow melting invisibly
from underneath, birds flying north at night
so high overhead that no one
could hear their cries—except, perhaps,
some man pulling on his boots at the back door
in the cold before dawn, going off to catch smelts
on the incoming tide.

Kate Barnes

Swans Mating

Even now I wish that you had been there
Sitting beside me on the riverbank:
The cob and his pen sailing in rhythm
Until their small heads met and the final
Heraldic moment dissolved in ripples.

This was a marriage and a baptism,
A holding of breath, nearly a drowning,
Wings spread wide for balance where he trod,
Her feathers full of water and her neck
Under the water like a bar of light.

Michael Longley

A nightingale

(poem fragment)

A nightingale
means
Spring's just about
here
her voice wanting
love

Sappho

*Translated from the ancient Greek
by Robert Bagg*

Song on May Morning

Now the bright morning-star, day's harbinger,
Comes dancing from the East, and leads with her
The flowery May, who from her green lap throws
The yellow cowslip and the pale primrose.
Hail, bounteous May, that does inspire
Mirth, and youth, and warm desire!
Woods and groves are of thy dressing;
Hill and dale doth boast thy blessing.
Thus we salute thee with our early song,
And welcome thee, and wish thee long.

John Milton

The Son

Ah son, do you know, do you know
where you come from?

From a lake with seagulls
white and hungry.

Near the winter water
she and I raised
a red bonfire
wearing out our lips
from kissing the soul,
casting all into the fire
burning our life.

That's how you came to the world.

But she, to see me
and to see you, one day
crossed the oceans,
and I, to hold
her small waist,
wandered all the earth,
across wars and mountains,
through sand and thorns.

That's how you came to the world.

You come from so many places,
from water and earth,
from fire and snow,
you walk from far away

toward us two,
from the terrible love
that has bewitched us,
so we want to know
what you're like, what you say to us,
because you know more
of the world we gave you.

Like a great storm
we shake
the tree of life
to its most hidden
root fibers
and you appear now
singing in the foliage,
in the highest branch
we reach with you.

Pablo Neruda

Translated from the Spanish
by Alison Sparks and Ilan Stavans

Love's Philosophy

The fountains mingle with the river
And the rivers with the ocean,
The winds of heaven mix for ever
With a sweet emotion;
Nothing in the world is single,
All things by a law divine
In one another's being mingle—
Why not I with thine?

See the mountains kiss high heaven,
And the waves clasp one another;
No sister-flower would be forgiven
If it disdain'd its brother:
And the sunlight clasps the earth,
And the moonbeams kiss the sea—
What are all these kissings worth,
If thou kiss not me?

Percy Bysshe Shelley

The Planned Child

I hated the fact that they had planned me, she had taken
a cardboard out of his shirt from the laundry
as if sliding the backbone up out of his body,
and made a chart of the month and put
her temperature on it, rising and falling,
to know the day to make me—I would have
liked to have been conceived in heat,
in haste, by mistake, in love, in sex,
not on cardboard, the little x on the
rising line that did not fall again.

But when a friend was pouring wine
and said that I seem to have been a child who had been wanted,
I took the wine against my lips
as if my mouth were moving along
that valved wall in my mother's body, she was
bearing down, and then breathing from the mask, and then
bearing down, pressing me out into
the world that was not enough for her without me in it,
not the moon, the sun, Orion
cartwheeling across the dark, not
the earth, the sea—none of it
was enough, for her, without me.

Sharon Olds

The Best Thing in the World

What's the best thing in the world?
June-rose, by May-dew impearled;
Sweet south-wind, that means no rain;
Truth, not cruel to a friend;
Pleasure, not in haste to end;
Beauty, not self-decked and curled
Till its pride is over-plain;
Light, that never makes you wink;
Memory, that gives no pain;
Love, when, so, you're loved again.
What's the best thing in the world?
—Something out of it, I think.

Elizabeth Barrett Browning

Putting in the Seed

You come to fetch me from my work tonight
When supper's on the table, and we'll see
If I can leave off burying the white
Soft petals fallen from the apple tree
(Soft petals, yes, but not so barren quite,
Mingled with these, smooth bean and wrinkled pea),
And go along with you ere you lose sight
Of what you came for and become like me,
Slave to a springtime passion for the earth.
How Love burns through the Putting in the Seed
On through the watching for that early birth
When, just as the soil tarnishes with weed,
The sturdy seedling with arched body comes
Shouldering its way and shedding the earth crumbs.

Robert Frost

Maybe All This

Maybe all this
is happening in some lab?
Under one lamp by day
and billions by night?

Maybe we're experimental generations?
Poured from one vial to the next,
shaken in test tubes,
not scrutinized by eyes alone,
each of us separately
plucked up by tweezers in the end?

Or maybe it's more like this:
No interference?
The changes occur on their own
according to plan?
The graph's needle slowly etches
its predictable zigzags?

Maybe thus far we aren't of much interest?
The control monitors aren't usually plugged in?
Only for wars, preferably large ones,
for the odd ascent above our clump of Earth,
for major migrations from point A to B?

Maybe just the opposite:
They've got a taste for trivia up there?
Look! on the big screen a little girl
is sewing a button on her sleeve.
The radar shrieks,
the staff comes at a run.

What a darling little being
with its tiny heart beating inside it!
How sweet, its solemn
threading of the needle!
Someone cries enraptured:
Get the Boss,
tell him he's got to see this for himself!

Wisława Szymborska

Translated from the Polish by
Stanisław Barańczak and Clare Cavanagh

The Story Goes On

So this is the tale my mother told me
That tale that was much too dull to hold me
And this is the surge and the rush she said would show
Our story goes on
Oh, I was young I'd forgot that things outlive me
My goal was the kick that life would give me
And now like a joke something moves to let me know
Our story goes on
And all these things I feel and more
My mother's mother felt and hers before
A chain of life begun upon the shore of some dark sea has reached
    to me
And now I can see the chain extending
My child is next in a line that has no ending
And here am I feeling life that her child will feel when I'm long gone
And thus it is our story goes on
And on and on and on and on and on and on and on and on
And all these things I feel and more
My mother's mother felt and hers before
A chain of life begun upon the shore of some primordial sea has
    stretched through time to reach to me
And now I can see the chain extending
My child is next in a line that has no ending
And here am I feeling life that her child will feel when I'm long gone
Yes all that was is part of me as I am part of what's to be
And thus it is our story goes on
And on and on and on and on

Richard Maltby

Spell for Inviting-in the New Soul

Shy one,
small donkey, come forward.
Let world be cradle.

Fish drifting, enter weight gladly.
Trust passage.

If suffering will chant you,
if terror,
in pine dark, deer breathing.
In sea-bench's sorrow gills salt-light.
Know owl-cries your forelock.

Know leaf-scent, know cities, know rivers,
doorways stand open.
In ice-grip, know muskrat's strong swimming.
Let asking.

Let losing and breaking, let weather.
Let entrance entirely.
Desires bray sweet in the ladders of loudness.

Shy one, small donkey, trust hoof-fall.
Seeds wait to ride on your ankles,
five baskets
of apple sleep guardian.

The bridle placed heavy wears bell-sounds.
Agreeing come forward.

Jane Hirshfield

Expecting

Grave, my wife lies back, hands cross
her chest, while the doctor searches early
for your heartbeat, peach pit, unripe

plum—pulls out the world's worst
boom box, a Mr. Microphone, to broadcast
your mother's lifting belly.

The whoosh and bellows of mama's body
and beneath it: nothing. Beneath
the slow stutter of her heart: nothing.

The doctor trying again to find you, fragile
fern, snowflake. Nothing.
After, my wife will say, in fear,

impatient, she went beyond her body,
this tiny room, into the ether—
for now, we spelunk for you one last time

lost canary, miner of coal
and chalk, lungs not yet black—
I hold my wife's feet to keep her here—

and me—trying not to dive starboard
to seek you in the dark water. And there
it is: faint, an echo, faster and further

away than mother's, all beat box
and fuzzy feedback. You are like hearing
hip-hop for the first time—power

hijacked from a lamppost—all promise.
You couldn't sound better, break-
dancer, my favorite song bumping

from a passing car. You've snuck
into the club underage and stayed!
Only later, much, will your mother

begin to believe your drumming
in the distance—my Kansas City
and Congo Square, this jazz band

vamping on inside her.

Kevin Young

Cello Suite

Cello gripped in her open thighs,
        she turns the pegs,
                tunes the strings;
                        her fingers slowly take
        each note's pulse,
walk mellowing
        tenor timbres
                down the fingerboard
                        toward rasping
                                baritones.

In strokes as surely drawn,
        chest-filling as her breaths,
                she pulls a hot summer's reckoning—
passion's full weight
        borne down on her—
                through melodies
                        respectful
                                of her resilience.

A few bars from the end
        she gives in to jubilant
                vibrations
        in the part of her
that's now child.

The bow lifts
        lovers let go
                the suite stops.

Reliving the ardor
　　　　　she faces the music—
　　　　　　　　　a child-birthing solo
she's composing
　　　　　herself to play
　　　　　　　　　without any
　　　　　　　　　　　　　rehearsal at all.

Weeks later the lovers sit side
　　　　　by side on the brick steps
　　　　　　　　　of her parents' home;
　　　　　　　　　　　　　her sliding tears
　　　　　　　　　　　　　　　　　reflect her mother's
stare into the whorls
　　　　　of the washing machine,
　　　　　　　　　and her father's powerless eyes—
they watch their daughter
　　　　　growing beyond
　　　　　　　　　anyone's control.

Cheek to her cello's gnarled scroll,
　　　　　impulsive
　　　　　　　　　irretrievable love,
once wildly made, crests,
　　　　　then calmly overflows
　　　　　　　　　the cello's rosewood curves.

As she lifts her bow to the skies
　　　　　her lover's hand slides
　　　　　　　　　under her shoulder,
　　　　　　　　　　　　　her breasts lift
　　　　　　　　　　　　　　　　　to his passing forearm.

Silence, after music,
      awakens their child.
           They spread their palms
               over a nine-month belly
                  the boy troubles,
palpable feet
      pacing his world,
         gathering strength
            in a hush only he
can break with a note
      perfectly pitched
         to the cry
            that joined his journey to theirs.

                    Robert Bagg

III
Waiting

To love an other only for being

—"Relearning the Alphabet,"
Denise Levertov

The Beautiful

Three things there are more beautiful
Than any man could wish to see:
The first, it is a full-rigged ship
Sailing with all her sails set free;
The second, when the wind and sun
Are playing in a field of corn;
The third, a woman, young and fair,
Showing her child before it is born.

W. H. Davies

Never Again Would Birds' Song Be the Same

He would declare and could himself believe
That the birds there in all the garden round
From having heard the daylong voice of Eve
Had added to their own an oversound,
Her tone of meaning but without the words.
Admittedly an eloquence so soft
Could only have had an influence on birds
When call or laughter carried it aloft.
Be that as may be, she was in their song.
Moreover her voice upon their voices crossed
Had now persisted in the woods so long
That probably it never would be lost.
Never again would birds' song be the same.
And to do that to birds was why she came.

Robert Frost

Ordinary Miracle

I have mourned lost days
When I accomplished nothing of importance.
But not lately.
Lately under the lunar tide
Of a woman's ocean, I work
My own sea-change:
Turning grains of sand to human eyes.
I daydream after breakfast
While the spirit of egg and toast
Knits together a length of bone
As fine as a wheatstalk.
Later, as I postpone weeding the garden
I will make two hands
That may tend a hundred gardens.

I need ten full moons exactly
For keeping the animal promise.
I offer myself up: unsaintly, but
Transmuted anyway
By the most ordinary miracle.
I am nothing in this world beyond the things one woman does.
But here are eyes that once were pearls
And here is a second chance where there was none.

Barbara Kingsolver

The Sonogram

Only a few weeks ago, the sonogram of Jean's womb
resembled nothing so much
as a satellite-map of Ireland:

now the image
is so well-defined we can make out not only a hand
but a thumb;

on the road to Spiddal, a woman hitching a ride;
a gladiator in his net, passing judgement on the crowd.

Paul Muldoon

Relearning the Alphabet
(*excerpt*)

A

Joy—a beginning.   Anguish, ardor.
To relearn the ah! of knowing in unthinking
joy: the belovéd stranger lives.
Sweep up anguish as with a wing-tip,
brushing the ashes back to the fire's core.

B

To be. To love an other only for being.

Denise Levertov

Upon Seeing an Ultrasound Photo of an Unborn Child

Tadpole, it's not time yet to nag you
about college (though I have some thoughts
on that), baseball (ditto), or abstract
principles. Enjoy your delicious,
soupy womb-warmth, do some rolls and saults
(it'll be too crowded soon), delight in your early
dreams—which no one will attempt to analyze.
For now: may your toes blossom, your fingers
lengthen, your sexual organs grow (too soon
to tell which yet) sensitive, your teeth
form their buds in their forming jawbone, your already
booming heart expand (literally
now, metaphorically later); O your spine,
eyebrows, nape, knees, fibulae,
lungs, lips . . . But your soul,
dear child: I don't see it here, when
does that come in, whence? Perhaps God,
and your mother, and even I—we'll all contribute
and you'll learn yourself to coax it
from wherever: your soul, which holds your bones
together and lets you live
on earth.—Fingerling, sidecar, nubbin,
I'm waiting, it's me, Dad,
I'm out here. You already know
where Mom is. I'll see you more directly
upon arrival. You'll recognize
me—I'll be the tall-seeming, delighted
blond guy, and I'll have
your nose.

Thomas Lux

Expectancy

Japan Baptist Hospital, Kyoto

One by one, we shuffle in
and take a quiet seat beneath
admonitory posters. Here's
Mrs. Shimoda, who, to judge from
her pink, quilted jumper appliquéd
with rabbits, and a fuzzy, enormous purse
emblazoned with cartoon characters,

appears to be in some confusion
as to whether she's going to have a baby
or (a greater miracle) become one;
and here's sorrowful Mrs. Fukumoto,
who hasn't looked well in weeks. Of course
I'm guessing—I'm a newcomer here,
and as the nurse calls out each name

just a touch louder than necessary
in a kindly, patronizing singsong,
I flinch. Thermometer under tongue,
blood pressure measured, I can clearly see
a needle creeping on the hateful scale
where serene Mrs. Oh, five months along,
checks in at less than I at two.

Yet don't I, in fact, want to feel the weight
of waiting once again? The way
(years ago) each birthday took years to arrive . . .
Oh to be sixteen at last, to drive,
to come home past eleven! To loosen
the hold of parents who'd grown to fear

time as a thing they only got less of,
while you knew, yourself, it was stored within.

Too early, I know, I begin to imagine
how the baby turns in its own waiting room,
as restlessly as I now turn
a health-book page in a half-learned language:
Let's guard against (illegible);
Be sure to (illegible) *every day!*

But here's the man who can read it all:
the doctor—handsome, young, a bit proud,
as if the father of all our children—
billows in on a white, open-coated sail
and, bowing to us with nautical
briskness, takes the time to wish
the mates a benevolent good morning.

We murmur in kind; then, in a hush,
some dozen heads in unison
swivel to follow his form until
it vanishes behind a door.
Daily, I think, women just like us
are found normal there. Who shall be the first?
It's Mrs. Hino—although the nurse

has to call her twice, across the length
of eight abstracted months. She rises
slowly, resting, in a universal
gesture I've only begun to read,
one hand on the swell below her breasts
as though what's borne within
were here, and could be taken in her arms.

Mary Jo Salter

Evenings, a Tiger's Roar Is Friend

At last the cedar waxwings
come in late April rain for the pagoda

tree's seeds that have hung
slack all winter and once again

begin to swell. A mallard roots
with her orange beak a puddle

by a busy walkway, having traded
the over-crowded pond for a site

more dangerous still. The T'ang dynasty
second period veil of the day is

impenetrable. Beneath the sky
cage of my ribs, a son practices breathing.

Lisa Olstein

Seed Leaves

Homage to R.F.

Here something stubborn comes,
Dislodging the earth crumbs
And making crusty rubble.
It comes up bending double,
And looks like a green staple.
It could be seedling maple,
Or artichoke, or bean.
That remains to be seen.

Forced to make choice of ends,
The stalk in time unbends,
Shakes off the seed-case, heaves
Aloft, and spreads two leaves
Which still display no sure
And special signature.
Toothless and fat, they keep
The oval form of sleep.

This plant would like to grow
And yet be embryo;
Increase, and yet escape
The doom of taking shape;
Be vaguely vast, and climb
To the tip end of time
With all of space to fill,
Like boundless Igdrasil
That has the stars for fruit.

But something at the root
More urgent than that urge

Bids two true leaves emerge,
And now the plant, resigned
To being self-defined
Before it can commerce
With the great universe,
Takes aim at all the sky
And starts to ramify.

Richard Wilbur

Infant

I needed motherhood like some nectar
from the gods. With the intoxication
of pride's unholy strength, I found it hard
to nurture the growing realization
that in a mother's hands all joy and terror
blossomed in this budding thing, and places
of no exit brought such painful error.
But because of their soft, petaled faces
we can accept our dark and shadowed side
where suffering rises unrelenting
right next to ecstasy, and we decide
that babies are the deep remembering
of what our strong desires can obscure,
how leaves break down so flowers can endure.

Susie Patlove

The Nursery

The baby
      was made in a cell
in the silver & rose underworld.
Invisibly prisoned
      in vessels & cords, no gold
for a baby; instead
eyes, and a sudden soul, twelve weeks
old, which widened its will.

Tucked in the notch of my fossil: bones
      laddered a spine from a cave,
the knees & skull
were etched in this cell, no stone, no gold
where no sun brushed its air.

One in one, we slept together
      all sculpture
           of two figures welded.
But the infant's fingers
squeezed & kneaded
        me, as if to show
the Lord won't crush what moves
on its own . . . secretly.

On Robeson Street
      anonymous
was best, where babies
have small hearts
      to learn
with;
    like intimate

thoughts on sea
water, they're limited.

Soldered to my self
        it might be a soldier or a thief
for all I know.
The line between revolution & crime
        is all in the mind
            where ideas of righteousness
and rights confuse.
I walked the nursery floor.
By four-eyed buttons & the curdle of a cradle's
paint: a trellis of old gold
        roses, lipped & caked
where feet will be kicking in wool.

                Then the running,
the race after,
cleaning the streets up for a life.
His technicolor cord
hung from a gallery of bones,
        but breathing *I'm finished.*
Both of us.

And when the baby sighed,
through his circle of lips,
                I kissed it,
        and so did he, my circle to his,
we kissed ourselves and each other,
        as if each cell was a Cupid,
and we were born to it.

The cornerstone's dust
upfloating

by trucks & tanks.
White flowers spackle

the sky crossing the sea.
A plane above the patio

wakes the silence
and my infant who raises

his arms to see
what he's made of.

O animation! O liberty!

                Fanny Howe

Expect Nothing

Expect nothing. Live frugally
On surprise.
Become a stranger
To need of pity
Or, if compassion be freely
Given out
Take only enough
Stop short of urge to plead
Then purge away the need.

Wish for nothing larger
Than your own small heart
Or greater than a star;
Tame wild disappointment
With caress unmoved and cold
Make of it a parka
For your soul.

Discover the reason why
So tiny human giant
Exists at all
So scared unwise
But expect nothing. Live frugally
On surprise.

Alice Walker

IV
Birth Day

Love set you going like a fat gold watch

—"Morning Song,"
Sylvia Plath

A Birthday

My heart is like a singing bird
Whose nest is in a water'd shoot;
My heart is like an apple-tree
Whose boughs are bent with thickset fruit;
My heart is like a rainbow shell
That paddles in a halcyon sea;
My heart is gladder than all these
Because my love is come to me.

Raise me a dais of silk and down;
Hang it with vair and purple dyes;
Carve it in doves and pomegranates,
And peacocks with a hundred eyes;
Work it in gold and silver grapes,
In leaves and silver fleurs-de-lys;
Because the birthday of my life
Is come, my love is come to me.

Christina Rossetti

Labor Night

Her world is upside down,
waiting for the baby.
She paces in the night
and sleeps the day.
She has cleaned every corner
of the house,
rearranged things twice,
then started on the garage.
Her belly so round,
so full of grace,
she cannot feel her legs
or in between them.
All this will have to wait.

For him there is nothing romantic
in the coming.
When there's not one
more inch to spare,
one more ounce of air,
he'll push his way
into the new world.

For now,
there is still time
between the violent seconds.
She rises in the night,
to cook the peppers,
pops the stems and scatters seeds,
and marvels at their colors—
yellow, orange, red and green.
Christmas in the air!

But life starts with a fight,
a gritting of his will
and single-mindedness.
Necessity, the mother of invention.
For his first breath,
he parts her bone,
slow and hard
like the resurrection,
and moving of the stone.

Susan Dane

First Birth

I had thought so little, really, of *her*,
inside me, all that time, not breathing—
intelligent, maybe curious,
her eyes closed. When the vagina opened,
slowly, from within, from the top, my eyes
rounded in shock and awe, it was like being
entered for the first time, but entered
from the inside, the child coming in
from the other world. Enormous, stately,
she was pressed through the channel, she turned, and rose,
they held her up by a very small ankle,
she dangled indigo and scarlet, and spread
her arms out in this world. Each thing
I did, then, I did for the first
time, touched the flesh of our flesh,
brought the tiny mouth to my breast,
she drew the avalanche of milk
down off the mountain, I felt as if
I was nothing, no one, I was everything to her, I was hers.

Sharon Olds

Cesarean

The surgeon with his unapologetic
blade parted darkness, revealing
day. Then from her large clay
he drew toward his masked
face my small clay. The clatter,
the white light, the vast freedom
were terrible. Outside in, oh, inside
out, and why did everybody shout?

Jane Kenyon

Giving birth was the funniest

Giving birth was the funniest.
"Go," said the grumpy nurse
and vaguely waved
in the direction down the hallway.
I grabbed my belly and went.
Walked and walked, then saw
a mirror, and in it a belly
dressed in a shirt up to the navel,
on thin shaky legs
the color of lilac . . .
Laughed for about five minutes.
Five minutes later gave birth.

Vera Pavlova

*Translated from the Russian
by Steven Seymour*

Adopting David, June 1, 1974

I just gave birth to a son,
I yell to the desk clerk
in Vermont, the birth
delivered by phone at 7 a.m.

a son, I call
through the door
to my husband
who is asleep

and we hold each other
like children
for the last time
childless

dress in shorts and boots
grin over waffles
fill ourselves with juice

and hike through the valley
where the men plant
their dark patches
with seed

we climb up through spring
up the granite mountain
just breaking water
giving life to what it bears
each year.

Judith Steinbergh

"In the Realm of the Mothers"
for Elizabeth Coatsworth Barnes

When I was twenty-three, I got up in the morning
peculiarly dizzy, and thought, "I can't be
pregnant, I'm not educated, I've never even
learned German!"
                But I was.
In the hospital I watched my roommate
unwrap her child and count his fingers and toes
so I unwrapped my own child, and counted
her fingers and toes. Then what? The tiny thing
lay wrapped again in her receiving blanket,
like a candy baby. She had a name
already, "Elizabeth," taken from my mother
and great-grandmother, and many more women
in a file behind them that receded
slowly backward into the blue
of time, their heavily-folded skirts
hanging like silent bells. The baby
slept, and I tentatively
sketched the crushed-looking planes
of her bruised new face, the stripes
of her pink blanket. While I gazed at her,
her cells were dividing invisibly, she was growing
steadily forward. She smelled of clean cotton, talcum,
and her own new flesh; I longed to sniff her
all over, like a dog with its puppy.
                      The nurse,
starched and crackling, guided my nipple
into that weak mouth whose first sips
encouraged the secret mind of the breasts
to give more, make more, teach me from inside

a new feeling that melted through me and startled me
like a shot of whiskey. I looked up
from the wrinkled infant face, and my eyes wandered
past florists' carnations, through the plateglass window,
and on over lined-up roofs, to rest
on a frieze of bare blue mountains receding
into the summer sky, fold
after unfathomable fold.

Kate Barnes

Morning Song

Love set you going like a fat gold watch.
The midwife slapped your footsoles, and your bald cry
Took its place among the elements.

Our voices echo, magnifying your arrival. New statue.
In a drafty museum, your nakedness
Shadows our safety. We stand round blankly as walls.

I'm no more your mother
Than the cloud that distils a mirror to reflect its own slow
Effacement at the wind's hand.

All night your moth-breath
Flickers among the flat pink roses. I wake to listen:
A far sea moves in my ear.

One cry, and I stumble from bed, cow-heavy and floral
In my Victorian nightgown.
Your mouth opens clean as a cat's. The window square

Whitens and swallows its dull stars. And now you try
Your handful of notes;
The clear vowels rise like balloons.

Sylvia Plath

Psalm 8

O Lord our Lord, how excellent is thy name in all the earth! Who hast
　　set thy glory above the heavens.

Out of the mouth of babes and sucklings hast thou
　　ordained strength because of thine enemies, that thou
　　mightest still the enemy and the avenger.

When I consider thy heavens, the work of thy fingers, the moon and
　　the stars, which thou hast ordained;

What is man, that thou art mindful of him? And the son of man, that
　　thou visitest him?

For thou hast made him a little lower than the angels, and hast
　　crowned him with glory and honour.

Thou madest him to have dominion over the works of thy hands; thou
　　hast put all things under his feet:

All sheep and oxen, yea, and the beasts of the field;

The fowl of the air, and the fish of the sea, and whatsoever passeth
　　through the paths of the seas.

O Lord our Lord, how excellent is thy name in all the earth!

The Bible, King James Version

A Newborn Girl at Passover

Consider one apricot in a basket of them.
It is very much like all the other apricots—
an individual already, skin and seed.

Now think of this day. One you will probably forget.
The next breath you take, a long drink of air.
Holiday or not, it doesn't matter.

A child is born and doesn't know what day it is.
The particular joy in my heart she cannot imagine.
The taste of apricots is in store for her.

Nan Cohen

The Video

When Laura was born, Ceri watched.
They all gathered around Mum's bed—
Dad and the midwife and Mum's sister
and Ceri. "Move over a bit," Dad said—
he was trying to focus the camcorder
on Mum's legs and the baby's head.

After she had a little sister,
and Mum had gone back to being thin,
and was twice as busy, Ceri played
the video again and again.
She watched Laura come out, and then,
in reverse, she made her go back in.

Fleur Adcock

She Will Gather Roses

A Tsimshian Lullaby for Girls

This little girl
only born to
gather wild roses.
Only born to
shake the wild rice loose
with her little fingers.
Only to collect the sap
of young hemlocks
in spring. This woman-
child was only born
to pick strawberries,
fill baskets with
blueberries, soapberries,
elderberries. This
little girl was
only born to
gather wild roses.

My Sun!

A Tewa Prayer

My Sun!
My Morning Star!
Help this child to become a man.
I name him
Rain-dew Falling!
I name him
Star Mountain!

Little Fanfare for Felix Magowan

Up beyond sense and praise,
There at the highest trumpet-blast
Of Fahrenheit, the sun is a great friend.
He is so brilliant and so warm!
Yet when his axle smokes and the spokes blaze
And he founders in dusk (or seems to),
Remember: he cannot change. It's earth, it's time,
Whose child you now are, quietly
Blotting him out. In the blue stare you raise
To your mother and father already the miniature,
Merciful, and lifelong eclipse,
Felix, has taken place;
The black pupil rimmed with rays
Contracted to its task—
That of revealing by obscuring
The sunlike friend behind it.
Unseen by you, may he shine back always
From what you see, from others. So welcome, friend.
Welcome to earth, time, others; to
These cool darks, of sense, of language,
Each at once thread and maze.
Finally welcome, if you like, to this
James your father's mother's father's younger son
Contrived with love for you
During your first days.

James Merrill

Ecce Puer

Of the dark past
A child is born;
With joy and grief
My heart is torn.

Calm in his cradle
The living lies.
May love and mercy
Unclose his eyes!

Young life is breathed
On the glass;
The world that was not
Comes to pass.

A child is sleeping:
An old man gone.
O, father forsaken,
Forgive your son!

James Joyce

Her First Calf

Her fate seizes her and brings her
down. She's heavy with it. It
wrings her. The great weight
is heaved out of her. It eases.
She moves into what she has become,
sure in her fate now
as a fish free in the current.
She turns to the calf who has broken
out of the womb's water and its veil.
He breathes. She licks his wet hair.
He gathers his legs under him
and rises. He stands, and his legs
wobble. After the months
of his pursuit of her, now
they meet face to face.
From the beginnings of the world
his arrival and her welcome
have been prepared. They have always
known each other.

Wendell Berry

The Pasture

I'm going out to clean the pasture spring;
I'll only stop to rake leaves away
(And wait to watch the water clear, I may):
I shan't be gone long.—You come too.

I'm going out to fetch the little calf
That's standing by the mother. It's so young
It totters when she licks it with her tongue.
I shan't be gone long.—You come too.

Robert Frost

A Cradle Song

The angels are stooping
Above your bed;
They weary of trooping
With the whimpering dead.

God's laughing in Heaven
To see you so good;
The Sailing Seven
Are gay with His mood.

I sigh that kiss you,
For I must own
That I shall miss you
When you have grown.

William Butler Yeats

V

Newest Child

while they named the story

it is his to write

—"Liam,"
Mary Jo Salter

Someone would like to have you for her child

Someone would like to have you for her child
but you are mine.
Someone would like to rear you on a costly mat
but you are mine.
Someone would like to place you on a camel blanket
but you are mine.
I have you to rear on a torn old mat.
Someone would like to have you as her child
but you are mine.

Akan Lullaby, African

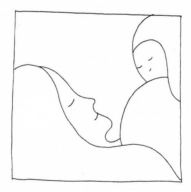

Waking with Russell

Whatever the difference is, it all began
the day we woke up face-to-face like lovers
and his four-day-old smile dawned on him again,
possessed him, till it would not fall or waver;
and I pitched back not my old hard-pressed grin
but his own smile, or one I'd rediscovered.
Dear son, I was *mezzo del cammin*
and the true path was as lost to me as ever
when you cut in front and lit it as you ran.
See how the true gift never leaves the giver:
returned and redelivered, it rolled on
until the smile poured through us like a river.
How fine, I thought, this waking amongst men!
I kissed your mouth and pledged myself forever.

Don Paterson

Only she who has breast-fed

Only she who has breast-fed
knows how beautiful the ear is.
Only they who have been breast-fed
know the beauty of the clavicle.
Only to humans the Creator
has given the earlobe.
The humans, through clavicles
slightly resembling birds,
entwined in caresses fly
to the place at night where,
rocking the cradle of cradles,
the babe is wailing,
where on a pillow of air
the stars nestle like toys.
And some of them speak.

Vera Pavlova

Translated from the Russian
by Steven Seymour

Infant Joy

"I have no name:
I am but two days old."
What shall I call thee?
"I happy am,
Joy is my name."
Sweet joy befall thee!

Pretty joy!
Sweet joy, but two days old.
Sweet Joy I call thee:
Thou dost smile,
I sing the while,
Sweet joy befall thee!

William Blake

Pale Twig

Eyes swollen from too little
sleep, I move quickly
toward your cry in the night
because you know only this instant,
because in your universe, eternity
passes in less than five minutes.
My hand cups
the back of your head,
a velvet bowl
whose newborn musk is the secret oil
I have no power over
as I bend
myself toward it again,

again. Your sobs fall away
as you drink at my breast,
like a brief dream
forgotten, and your small hand
slips along my arm, barely touching,
dancing in circles. Eyes closed,
you poke a finger
into my mouth, offering me
drink, and I pretend
to draw some milk from that pale
twig as you smile back,
eyes still closed,
getting the joke.

Sleep arrives and your bird-like
frame of bone breathes
almost invisibly, yet

I no longer check for the mist
of your breath with one finger.
After hours, timeless
hours, holding you within
and now with
the shell of my body, I finally
trust breath
to keep breathing you
into your life.

Chivas Sandage

Baby Song

From the private ease of Mother's womb
I fall into the lighted room.

Why don't they simply put me back
Where it is warm and wet and black?

But one thing follows on another.
Things were different inside Mother.

Padded and jolly I would ride
The perfect comfort of her inside.

They tuck me in a rustling bed
—I lie there, raging, small, and red.

I may sleep soon, I may forget,
But I won't forget that I regret.

A rain of blood poured round her womb,
But all time roars outside this room.

                    Thom Gunn

Bathing the New Born

I love with an almost fearful love
to remember the first baths I gave him—
our second child, our first son—
I laid the little torso along
my left forearm, nape of the neck
in the crook of my elbow, hips nearly as
small as a least tern's hips
against my wrist, thigh held loosely
in the loop of thumb and forefinger, the
sign that means exactly right. I'd soap him,
the long, violet, cold feet,
the scrotum wrinkled as a waved whelk shell
so new it was flexible yet, the chest,
the hands, the clavicles, the throat, the gummy
furze of the scalp. When I got him too soapy he'd
slide in my grip like an armful of buttered
noodles, but I'd hold him not too tight,
I felt that I was good for him,
I'd tell him about his wonderful body
and the wonderful soap, and he'd look up at me,
one week old, his eyes still wide
and apprehensive. I love that time
when you croon and croon to them, you can see
the calm slowly entering them, you can
sense it in your clasping hand,
the little spine relaxing against
the muscle of your forearm, you feel the fear

leaving their bodies, he lay in the blue
oval plastic baby tub and
looked at me in wonder and began to
move his silky limbs at will in the water.

Sharon Olds

Little Feet

Little feet, too young and soft to walk,
Little lips, too young and pure to talk.

My baby has a mottled fist,
My baby has a neck in creases;
My baby kisses and is kissed,
For he's the very thing for kisses.

Christina Rossetti

For Benjamin, Beloved Son

I

For you I have built a cradle,
piecing it awkwardly, day after day,
mistaken in measure,
saw skipping, hammerblows
wide of the mark,
yet, look, it rocks
and you sleep sound!

II

Since you burst squalling into this world
I've watched flesh thicken on your bone.
Your eyes, at first unfocused,
have slowly sharpened into sight,
the pupils pinpoints of the darkness whence you came
the rest all light.

And now you trace my movements as I dance.
Plump and bright you gurgle from your chair,
tickled to see your father so foolish,
sporting to make you laugh,
big hands winnowing air.

My son, for you I'd dance forever,
heels on fire,
and only bend from time to time
to kiss your still soft crown

and cup your chin and silken cheeks
between my trembling palms.

III

No tortoise likes being on his back
nor you, little turtle,
bowed legs striking the air,
hands balled and beating.
You howl with indignation—
diaper, powder, and pins—
and will not relent.
I hurry, minding the pricks,
shamed by your squalling
and sorry. Yet what else?
You must be changed.

Done, I raise you, hand behind head,
and hug you quiet.
Worse things have happened to babies,
and even a turtle forgets.

                    Thomas Yeomans

For Joshua, One Month Old

Joshua, your hands and fingers
Are so light and small
That when you fall asleep
You rest them on the air.
Gravity has no hold on them
And has to leave them there.

Anne Porter

Lullaby and Good Night

Lullaby and good night, with roses bedight
With lilies o'er spread is baby's wee bed
Lay thee down now and rest, may thy slumber be blessed
Lay thee down now and rest, may thy slumber be blessed

Lullaby and good night, thy mother's delight
Bright angels beside my darling abide
They will guard thee at rest, thou shalt wake on my breast
They will guard thee at rest, thou shalt wake on my breast

Johannes Brahms
Translator unknown

Five Tanka

Hospital visit
grandmothers discuss
the color
of the newborn's
closed eyes

Daffodils
because tomorrow
the sun
will shine on the face
of this newborn

Butterfly here . . . there . . .
My small daughter—never sure
when she lifts a foot just
where she will again touch earth
The lightness of her days

In the blizzard
I teach my daughter to make
a snow angel—
she promises
to be good forever

The ballad
of a long-ago princess . . .
the children's eyes wide
with the splendor of that world
a poet weaves for them

Carol Purington

Summer 1983

None of us remembers these, the days
when passing strangers adored us at first sight,
just for living, or for strolling down the street;
praised all our given names; begged us to smile . . .
you, too, in a little while,
my darling, will have lost all this,
asked for a kiss will give one, and learn
how love dooms us to earn
love once we can speak of it.

Mary Jo Salter

Mutterings over the Crib of a Deaf Child

"How will he hear the bell at school
Arrange the broken afternoon,
And know to run across the cool
Grasses where the starlings cry,
Or understand the day is gone?"

Well, someone lifting curious brows
Will take the measure of the clock.
And he will see the birchen boughs
Outside sagging dark from the sky,
And the shade crawling upon the rock.

"And how will he know to rise at morning?
His mother has other sons to waken,
She has the stove she must build to burning
Before the coals of the nighttime die;
And he never stirs when he is shaken."

I take it the air affects his skin,
And you remember, when you were young,
Sometimes you could feel the dawn begin,
And the fire would call you, by and by,
Out of the bed and bring you along.

"Well, good enough. To serve his needs
All kinds of arrangements can be made.
But what will you do if his finger bleeds?
Or a bobwhite whistles invisibly
And flutes like an angel off in the shade?"

He will learn pain. And, as for the bird,
It is always darkening when that comes out.
I will putter as though I had not heard,
And lift him into my arms and sing
Whether he hears my song or not.

James Wright

My Little One

My little one whose tongue is dumb,
whose fingers cannot hold to things,
who is so mercilessly young,
he leaps upon the instant things,

I hold him not. Indeed, who could?
He runs into the burning wood.
Follow, follow if you can!
He will come out grown to a man

and not remember whom he kissed,
who caught him by the slender wrist
and bound him by a tender yoke
which, understanding not, he broke.

Tennessee Williams

Mary's song

Blue homespun and the bend of my breast
keep warm this small hot naked star
fallen to my arms. (Rest . . .
you who have had so far
to come.) Now nearness satisfies
the body of God sweetly. Quiet he lies
whose vigor hurled
a universe. He sleeps
whose eyelids have not closed before.

His breath (so slight it seems
no breath at all) once ruffled the dark deeps
to sprout a world.
Charmed by dove's voices, the whisper of straw,
he dreams,
hearing no music from his other spheres.
Breath, mouth, ears, eyes
he is curtailed
who overflowed all skies,
all years.
Older than eternity, now he
is new. Now native to earth as I am, nailed
to my poor planet, caught that I might be free,
blind in my womb to know my darkness ended,
brought to this birth
for me to be new-born,
and for him to see me mended
I must see him torn.

Luci Shaw

93

Liam

He's down again, aswim in a dream
of milk, and Teresa who is far
too tired to go back to sleep goes back
to the table where she tests the nib
of her pen, like the nipple on a bottle.

Into a bottle of permanent ink
she dips her pen and begins to trace
over her pencil-marks on the face
of the spiral scrapbook the name they chose
for him who has never dreamed of a name.

It's *William,* like his father, but
she has only got as far as *Will*
(the doubled *l* another spiral
to the *Liam* they now call him), which
leaves her still three letters to spell

the man who's curled up in *I am.*
—The stranger in the crib who seems
longer each time they lift him out
and will find that while they named the story
it is his to write.

Mary Jo Salter

Pre-Text

(for Douglas, at one)

Archaic, his gestures
hieratic, just like Caesar or Sappho
or Mary's Jesus or Ann's Mary or Jane
Austen once, or me or your mother's you

the sudden baby surges to his feet
and sways, head forward, chin high,
arms akimbo, hands dangling idle,
elbows up, as if winged.

The features of his face stand out
amazed, all eyes as his aped posture
sustains him aloft
                    a step a step a rush
and he walks,

Young Anyone, his lifted point of view
far beyond the calendar.

What time is it? Firm in time
he is out of date—

like a cellarer for altar wines
tasting many summers in one glass,

or like a grandmother
in whose womb her
granddaughter once
slept in egg inside
grandma's unborn daughter's
folded ovaries.

Marie Ponsot

On Children

Your children are not your children.
They are the sons and daughters of Life's longing for itself.
They come through you but not from you,
And though they are with you yet they belong not to you.

You may give them your love but not your thoughts,
For they have their own thoughts.
You may house their bodies but not their souls,
For their souls dwell in the house of tomorrow,
Which you cannot visit, not even in your dreams.
You may strive to be like them,
But seek not to make them like you.
For life goes not backward nor tarries with yesterday.

You are the bows from which your children
As living arrows are sent forth.
The archer sees the mark upon the path of the infinite,
And He bends you with His might
That His arrows may go swift and far.
Let your bending in the archer's hand be for gladness;
For even as He loves the arrow that flies,
So He loves also the bow that is stable.

Kahlil Gibran

VI
Sleep and Song

So when night is come, and you have gone to bed,
All the songs you love to sing shall echo in your head

—"Come, My Little Children, Here Are Songs for You,"
Robert Louis Stevenson

Dusk

(poem fragment)

Dusk you

fetch everything

dawn scatters

you fetch a lamb   a kid

you fetch a mother

her child

Sappho

Translated from the ancient Greek
by Robert Bagg

The Jackson Song

Little blue dreamer go to sleep
Let's close our eyes and call the deep
Slumbering land that just begins
When day is done and little dreamers spin

First take my hand now let it go
Little blue boy you're on your own
Little blue wings as those feet fly
Little blue shoes that walk across the sky

May your path be your own
But I'm with you
And each day you'll grow
He'll be there too
And someday when you go
We'll follow you
As you go, as you go

Little blue star that offers light
Little blue bird that offers flight
Little blue path where those feet fall
Little blue dreamer won't you dream it all

Refrain
And in your travels you will see
Warrior wings remember Daddy
And if a mama bird you see
Folding her wings will you remember me
As you go, as you go
As you go, as you go

Patti Smith

Come, My Little Children, Here Are Songs for You

Come, my little children, here are songs for you;
Some are short and some are long, and all, all are new.
You must learn to sing them very small and clear,
Very true to time and tune and pleasing to the ear.

Mark the note that rises, mark the notes that fall,
Mark the time when broken, and the swing of it all.
So when night is come, and you have gone to bed,
All the songs you love to sing shall echo in your head.

Robert Louis Stevenson

Music

Let me go where'er I will,
I hear a sky-born music still:
It sounds from all things old,
It sounds from all things young,
From all that's fair, from all that's foul,
Peals out a cheerful song.

It is not only in the rose,
It is not only in the bird,
Not only where the rainbow glows,
Nor in the song of woman heard,
But in the darkest, meanest things
There alway, alway something sings.

'T is not in the high stars alone,
Nor in the cup of budding flowers,
Nor in the redbreast's mellow tone,
Nor in the bow that smiles in showers,
But in the mud and scum of things
There alway, alway something sings.

Ralph Waldo Emerson

Vespers

Little Boy kneels at the foot of the bed,
Droops on the little hands little gold head.
Hush! Hush! Whisper who dares!
Christopher Robin is saying his prayers.

God bless Mummy. I know that's right.
Wasn't it fun in the bath to-night?
The cold's so cold, and the hot's so hot.
Oh! *God bless Daddy*—I quite forgot.

If I open my fingers a little bit more,
I can see Nanny's dressing-gown on the door.
It's a beautiful blue, but it hasn't a hood.
Oh! *God bless Nanny and make her good.*

Mine has a hood, and I lie in bed,
And pull the hood right over my head,
And I shut my eyes, and I curl up small,
And nobody knows that I'm there at all.

Oh! *Thank you, God, for a lovely day.*
And what was the other I had to say?
I said "Bless Daddy," so what can it be?
Oh! Now I remember it. *God bless Me.*

Little Boy kneels at the foot of the bed,
Droops on the little hands little gold head.
Hush! Hush! Whisper who dares!
Christopher Robin is saying his prayers.

A. A. Milne

Emily Wants to Play

That alarming cry—
and before I even understand
I'm up, I've stumbled down the hall
to where she lies in wait on her back,
smiling. She's fooled me again.
By the digital clock
it's 2:53 in the morning, and
Emily wants to play.

She rustles in
sheer happiness, under quilts I peel
back to take her up, up,
and into the crook of my arm,
where she's far too thrilled to settle.
She wants no bottle,
shrugs off my gentle rocking—no,
she'd rather squirm

to face those two
red eyes dividing hour from minute,
staring at hers as if they know
how blue they'll grow by day.
As she turns to me
I look away,
with a heavy nod to illustrate
We're sleeping now, see?

But see she does,
her eyes a magnifying glass
to burn my eyes in shame: she's had
time already to learn

that nighttime is for love.
Wakefulness
touches me gladly now, the thought
of the giant yellow moon

the night she was born,
and later, come winter, how
I nursed her by the light of snow
ticking against this window.
Having won me at last,
she yawns; she's been vigilant
as this memory of her that can't
rest until set down.

Mary Jo Salter

Grown-up

Was it for this I uttered prayers,
And sobbed and cursed and kicked the stairs,
That now, domestic as a plate,
I should retire at half-past eight?

Edna St. Vincent Millay

Hush, Little Baby

Hush, little baby, don't say a word,
Papa's gonna buy you a mockingbird.

If that mockingbird don't sing,
Papa's gonna buy you a diamond ring.

If that diamond ring turns brass,
Papa's gonna buy you a looking glass.

If that looking glass gets broke,
Papa's gonna buy you a billy goat.

If that billy goat won't pull,
Papa's gonna buy you a cart and bull.

If that cart and bull turn over,
Papa's gonna buy you a dog named Rover.

If that dog named Rover don't bark,
Papa's gonna buy you a horse and cart.

If that horse and cart fall down,
You'll still be the sweetest little baby in town.

Traditional Folk Song

Siena, age 3 months

I carried my baby down the dark
road between the moon
and pond. She cried as if she wanted
some better balance
of light and water.

               I tried
to sing her what quiet
I could take from those places.
But she cried
as if she needed calm
from far below me,
below the search for balance,

                    deep

into rock, down where centers
meet, where I could no more
extract it than she would know
if she saw it. As if she knew
I could grasp at the loss
as ballast against falling
or floating any sudden way.

               Or

that I could hold her close
against both our uneven places
and sway and sway and sway and sway.

          Michael Chrisman

Sweet and Low

Sweet and low, sweet and low,
  Wind of the western sea,
Low, low, breathe and blow,
  Wind of the western sea!
Over the rolling waters go,
  Come from the dying moon, and blow,
Blow him again to me;
  While my little one, while my pretty one sleeps.

Sleep and rest, sleep and rest,
  Father will come to thee soon;
Rest, rest, on mother's breast,
  Father will come to thee soon;
Father will come to his babe in the nest,
  Silver sails all out of the west
Under the silver moon:
  Sleep, my little one, sleep, my pretty one, sleep.

Alfred, Lord Tennyson

A Child Asleep

How he sleepeth! having drunken
Weary childhood's mandragore,
From his pretty eyes have sunken
Pleasures, to make room for more—
Sleeping near the withered nosegay, which he pulled the day before.

Nosegays! leave them for the waking:
Throw them earthward where they grew.
Dim are such, beside the breaking
Amaranths he looks unto—
Folded eyes see brighter colours than the open ever do.

Heaven-flowers, rayed by shadows golden
From the paths they sprang beneath,
Now perhaps divinely holden,
Swing against him in a wreath—
We may think so from the quickening of his bloom and of his
        breath.

Vision unto vision calleth,
While the young child dreameth on.
Fair, O dreamer, thee befalleth
With the glory thou hast won!
Darker wert thou in the garden, yestermorn, by summer sun.

We should see the spirits ringing
Round thee,—were the clouds away.
'Tis the child-heart draws them, singing
In the silent-seeming clay—
Singing!—Stars that seem the mutest, go in music all the way.

As the moths around a taper,
As the bees around a rose,
As the gnats around a vapour,—
So the Spirits group and close
Round about a holy childhood, as if drinking its repose.

Shapes of brightness overlean thee,—
Flash their diadems of youth
On the ringlets which half screen thee,—
While thou smilest, . . . not in sooth
Thy smile . . . but the overfair one, dropt from some aethereal mouth.

Haply it is angels' duty,
During slumber, shade by shade:
To fine down this childish beauty
To the thing it must be made,
Ere the world shall bring it praises, or the tomb shall see it fade.

Softly, softly! make no noises!
Now he lieth dead and dumb—
Now he hears the angels' voices
Folding silence in the room—
Now he muses deep the meaning of the Heaven-words as they come.

Speak not! he is consecrated—
Breathe no breath across his eyes.
Lifted up and separated,
On the hand of God he lies,
In a sweetness beyond touching—held in cloistral sanctities.

Could ye bless him—father—mother?
Bless the dimple in his cheek?

Dare ye look at one another,
And the benediction speak?
Would ye not break out in weeping, and confess yourselves too weak?

He is harmless—ye are sinful,—
Ye are troubled—he, at ease:
From his slumber, virtue winful
Floweth outward with increase—
Dare not bless him! but be blessed by his peace—and go in peace.

Elizabeth Barrett Browning

Kiss Her Dreaming

Bright plastic people, tall
as a finger, perch in laps of monkeys,
lambs, bears and babies that live
on my daughter's pillow. They stare
me right in the eye as I quickly
move them aside with one arm
while the other holds her sleeping
four-year-old body, limp
legs dangling. I manage
to pull back her blanket only to reveal
another battalion of small dolls sleeping side
by side, heads tucked tightly
under the sheet with no chance
of peeking heads out for a breath.

My arm's reach toward an efficient sweep
slows mid-air, becoming more respectful
of their persons—as if she's watching.
Laying her down, I'm stopped
by the smell of fine, brown hair,
must rub my thumb across
her cheek, smoothing
a place to kiss her dreaming
face. I stoop to plant that kiss as if
it will be absorbed into her
every bone, every cell. As if, though
she will not remember, she'll know.

Chivas Sandage

Behold This Little Bane

Behold this little Bane—
The Boon of all alive—
As common as it is unknown
The name of it is Love—

To lack of it is Woe—
To own of it is Wound—
Not elsewhere—if in Paradise
Its Tantamount be found—

Emily Dickinson

VII
At Play

as small as a world and as large as alone

—"maggie and milly and molly and may,"
E. E. Cummings

Spring Morning

Where am I going? I don't quite know.
Down to the stream where the king-cups grow—
Up on the hill where the pine trees blow—
Anywhere, anywhere. *I* don't know.

Where am I going? The clouds sail by,
Little ones, baby ones, over the sky.
Where am I going? The shadows pass,
Little ones, baby ones, over the grass.

If you were a cloud, and sailed up there,
You'd sail on water as blue as air,
And you'd see me here in the fields and say:
"Doesn't the sky look green to-day?"

Where am I going? The high rooks call:
"It's awful fun to be born at all."
Where am I going? The ring-doves coo:
"We do have beautiful things to do."

If you were a bird, and lived on high,
You'd lean on the wind when the wind came by,
You'd say to the wind when it took you away:
"*That's* where I wanted to go to-day!"

Where am I going? I don't quite know.
What does it matter where people go?
Down to the wood where the blue-bells grow—
Anywhere, anywhere. *I* don't know.

A. A. Milne

I May, I Might, I Must

If you will tell me why the fen
appears impassable, I then
will tell you why I think that I
can get across it if I try.

Marianne Moore

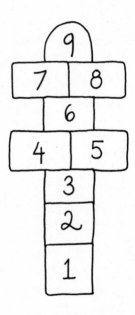

The Children's Hour

Between the dark and the daylight,
When the night is beginning to lower,
Comes a pause in the day's occupations,
That is known as the Children's Hour.

I hear in the chamber above me
The patter of little feet,
The sound of a door that is opened,
And voices soft and sweet.

From my study I see in the lamplight,
Descending the broad hall stair,
Grave Alice, and laughing Allegra,
And Edith with golden hair.

A whisper, and then a silence:
Yet I know by their merry eyes
They are plotting and planning together
To take me by surprise.

A sudden rush from the stairway,
A sudden raid from the hall!
By three doors left unguarded
They enter my castle wall!

They climb up into my turret
O'er the arms and back of my chair;
If I try to escape, they surround me;
They seem to be everywhere.

They almost devour me with kisses,
Their arms about me entwine,
Till I think of the Bishop of Bingen
In his Mouse-Tower on the Rhine!

Do you think, O blue-eyed banditti,
Because you have scaled the wall,
Such an old mustache as I am
Is not a match for you all!

I have you fast in my fortress,
And will not let you depart,
But put you down into the dungeon
In the round-tower of my heart.

And there will I keep you forever,
Yes, forever and a day,
Till the walls shall crumble to ruin,
And moulder in dust away!

       Henry Wadsworth Longfellow

Almost Six

for Lauren

I heard her say tonight to her mother
in secret whisper not to tell that she
loves her dad a lot, smile over shoulder,
"No! Don't tell!" as I approach, declaim, "Don't
tell *what*?" in my affected Villain Voice
meant for impish enjoyment as she skirls
and I Frankenstein-forward claws outstretched
gesturing to "tickle spots" under her
armpits: "*NO* Da-ddy!" entreats opposite
replete with giggles and taunts that cast me
in the role of monster/hero father
and I recall her fourth Christmas when I
intoned, "Tiger! Tiger! burning bright—" she
pistoled back, "Won't you guide my sleigh tonight!"

David Stanford Burr

Toys on the Planet Earth

We need carved wooden cows, kites,
small dolls with flexible limbs.
I vote for the sponge in the shape of a sandwich.
Keep your bad news, world.
Dream of something better.

A triangle mobile spinning in the wind.
Furry monkeys hugging.

When my dad was small,
his only toy was an acorn and a stick.
That's what he told me.
So he carved the acorn into a spinning top
and wrote in the dirt.
And that's what made him
the man he is today.

Naomi Shihab Nye

The Kitten and Falling Leaves

(excerpt)

That way look, my infant, lo!
What a pretty baby-show!
See the kitten on the wall,
Sporting with the leaves that fall,
Withered leaves—one—two—and three—
From the lofty elder-tree!

William Wordsworth

Only Child

1

I cradled my newborn daughter
and felt the heartbeat
pull me out of shock.
She didn't know
what her hands were:
she folded them. I asked her
was there a place
where there was no world.
She didn't know
what a voice was: her lips
were the shape of a nipple.

2

In the park the child says:
watch me. It will not count
unless you see. And she shows me
the cartwheel, the skip, the tumble,
the tricks performed at leisure in midair,
each unknown until it is finished.
At home she orders:
see me eat. I watch her
curl on herself, sleep;
as I try to leave the dark room
her dreaming voice commands me: watch.

3

Always we passed the seesaw
on the way to the swings
but tonight I remember
the principle of the lever,
I sit the child at one end,
I sit near the center,
the fulcrum, at once she has power
to lift me off the earth
and keep me suspended
by her tiny weight, she laughing,
I stunned at the power of the formula.

D. Nurkse

Children and All That Jazz

Little Annie Fannie
Morgan and Christian
Katy and Nathan
Tommy and Zem Zem
Alex and J.J.
Tai and Ezekial
Amy and Josie
Matthew and Mwosi
Sweet Pearl and Nicholas
Come here and tickle us
I don't like nicknames
I like to play games
One of them's Batman
That's where it's at man
Look at your t-shirt
I see you're all wet now
I'll give you a bath
If you'll go to bed now
Oh can't you see
I'm tired
I'm tired
I'm tired

Joey and Janet
Jennifer, Joshua
Justin and Jason
Jacob and Jordan
Heather and Shannon
Marisa and Kirsten
Kimmie and David

Who shall we play with?
Here comes my own son
Light of my life is
Younger than new leaves
Brighter than you please
Says that he loves me
Big as the world
And Gabriel Harris
You go to bed now
You go to bed now
It's quarter to nine
I'm tired
I'm tired
I'm tired

You heard what I said now
You go to bed now
It was a hard day
Never enough play
Iggy was sick
And couldn't come over
One of your mice died
That was when you cried
Get in the tub
And play with your boats now
Sit here beside me
I'll tell you a story
One about snakes
And anything gory
Ask me no questions
How far is the sky
And I'm falling asleep

And you're smarter than I am
Light of my life
Good night
Good night
Good night

Joan Baez

On Turning Ten

The whole idea of it makes me feel
like I'm coming down with something,
something worse than any stomach ache
or the headaches I get from reading in bad light—
a kind of measles of the spirit,
a mumps of the psyche,
a disfiguring chicken pox of the soul.

You tell me it is too early to be looking back,
but that is because you have forgotten
the perfect simplicity of being one
and the beautiful complexity introduced by two.
But I can lie on my bed and remember every digit.
At four I was an Arabian wizard.
I could make myself invisible
by drinking a glass of milk a certain way.
At seven I was a soldier, at nine a prince.

But now I am mostly at the window
watching the late afternoon light.
Back then it never fell so solemnly
against the side of my tree house,
and my bicycle never leaned against the garage
as it does today,
all the dark blue speed drained out of it.

This is the beginning of sadness, I say to myself,
as I walk through the universe in my sneakers.
It is time to say good-bye to my imaginary friends,
time to turn the first big number.

It seems only yesterday I used to believe
there was nothing under my skin but light.
If you cut me I would shine.
But now when I fall upon the sidewalks of life,
I skin my knees. I bleed.

Billy Collins

maggie and milly and molly and may

maggie and milly and molly and may
went down to the beach (to play one day)

and maggie discovered a shell that sang
so sweetly she couldn't remember her troubles,and

milly befriended a stranded star
whose rays five languid fingers were;

and molly was chased by a horrible thing
which raced sideways while blowing bubbles;and

may came home with a smooth round stone
as small as a world and as large as alone.

For whatever we lose (like a you or a me)
it's always ourselves we find in the sea

E. E. Cummings

Of All She Surveys

The day began as failure and became a field
with the wind blowing through.

Not empty: someone's laid out a blanket,

sun, bread, sky—even the fool
dog that jumps, upsetting the wine,

and at the bottom of the field, looking so small

I almost mistake them for rabbits,
my children.

As usual, she quit the game half-way,

and he—cheated, bereft—proceeds to fall apart.
But she dangles a crown, promises

buttercup, daisy, clover

and he brightens. I'm happy here, too,
watching the sun get lost

behind milkweed clouds, listening

to his grief evaporate and her song carry,
though I catch only half on the wind.

Song I taught her and forgot. Song she weaves.

Maybe I'm queen, maybe she is.
You'd think I'd get the difference

between descent and ascent,

dissent and assent.
After so much careful looking, looking

and refusing to look,

you'd think I'd know plenty—
that snake in the grass—when I see it.

Amy Dryansky

If I Can Stop One Heart from Breaking

If I can stop one Heart from breaking
I shall not live in vain
If I can ease one Life the Aching
Or cool one Pain

Or help one fainting Robin
Unto his Nest again
I shall not live in Vain.

Emily Dickinson

12 May 1996

Yes, we can loll here for six more chapters, before—yes,
waffles, yes you can stay naked all day or until you think
you need clothes, yes to butter on the video popcorn today
and me beside you for not just the scary parts, then yes
to a rain-walk, yes, even to the culvert rushing water and
the long way home, yes to candles with dinner, yes to no
lettuce, yes, I'll save the opera and switch to jazz, yes—
a bath bead?—take two, and yes I will sing the song, yes,
just this once, three times.

Ellen Doré Watson

Bright Days

Bright days, hand-in-hand—what a friendship we had then!
You said, "The river is shampooing its hair," and we played
Pooh sticks from its bridge.

that glint
    in the forest—
        where did it go?

Larry Kimmel

For Denis at Ten

He is a serious boy, a visitor.
He sees how an orchard of apple trees
opens this oriole morning
into a fossil-rock field where cattle
would stumble were there no rose-tangled
old walls of stone to hold them away.
Whistling, he is the serious city boy
who, given a country mission, strides
down the cow path, juggling a greening
to shy at recalcitrant rumps. He knows
he was sent. He goes on his own;
he takes into account
cows, chipmunk nutters, cowplats, sky!
& stones, holding each other into a wall,
and a black snake sunning, and, sky.

Birds slip brightness in among nettles and thistles.
It is early July. He was sent to the brook
beyond the pasture, for watercress.
He goes there, whistling.
                    Nothing reminds him of something.
He sees what is there to see.

                              Marie Ponsot

134

VIII

Green and Carefree

If they could, the trees would lift you

—"Pine Forest,"
Gabriela Mistral

Frost at Midnight

(excerpt)

Dear Babe, that sleepest cradled by my side,
Whose gentle breathings, heard in this deep calm,
Fill up the interspersèd vacancies
And momentary pauses of the thought!
My babe so beautiful! it thrills my heart
With tender gladness, thus to look at thee,
And think that thou shalt learn far other lore,
And in far other scenes! For I was reared
In the great city, pent 'mid cloisters dim,
And saw nought lovely but the sky and stars.
But thou, my babe! shalt wander like a breeze
By lakes and sandy shores, beneath the crags
Of ancient mountain, and beneath the clouds,
Which image in their bulk both lakes and shores
And mountain crags: so shalt thou see and hear
The lovely shapes and sounds intelligible
Of that eternal language, which thy God
Utters, who from eternity doth teach
Himself in all, and all things in himself.
Great universal Teacher! he shall mould
Thy spirit, and by giving make it ask.

Therefore all seasons shall be sweet to thee,
Whether the summer clothe the general earth
With greenness, or the redbreast sit and sing
Betwixt the tufts of snow on the bare branch
Of mossy apple-tree, while the nigh thatch
Smokes in the sun-thaw; whether the eave-drops fall

Heard only in the trances of the blast,
Or if the secret ministry of frost
Shall hang them up in silent icicles,
Quietly shining to the quiet Moon.

Samuel Taylor Coleridge

We Who Were Born

We who were born
In country places
Far from cities
And shifting faces,
We have a birthright
No man can sell,
And a shifting joy
No man can tell.

For we are kindred
To lordly things:
The wild duck's flight
And the white owl's wings,
The pike and the salmon,
The bull and the horse,
The curlew's cry
And the smell of gorse.

Pride of trees,
Swiftness of streams,
Magic of frost
Have shaped our dreams.
No baser vision
Their spirit fills
Who walk by right
On the naked hills.

Eiluned Lewis

Fern Hill

Now as I was young and easy under the apple boughs
About the lilting house and happy as the grass was green,
     The night above the dingle starry,
          Time let me hail and climb
     Golden in the heydays of his eyes,
And honoured among wagons I was prince of the apple towns
And once below a time I lordly had the trees and leaves
          Trail with daisies and barley
     Down the rivers of the windfall light.

And as I was green and carefree, famous among the barns
About the happy yard and singing as the farm was home,
     In the sun that is young once only,
          Time let me play and be
     Golden in the mercy of his means,
And green and golden I was huntsman and herdsman, the calves
Sang to my horn, the foxes on the hills barked clear and cold,
          And the sabbath rang slowly
     In the pebbles of the holy streams.

All the sun long it was running, it was lovely, the hay
Fields high as the house, the tunes from the chimneys, it was air
     And playing, lovely and watery
          And fire green as grass.
     And nightly under the simple stars
As I rode to sleep the owls were bearing the farm away,
All the moon long I heard, blessed among stables, the nightjars
     Flying with the ricks, and the horses
          Flashing into the dark.

And then to awake, and the farm, like a wanderer white
With the dew, come back, the cock on his shoulder: it was all
    Shining, it was Adam and maiden,
        The sky gathered again
    And the sun grew round that very day.
So it must have been after the birth of the simple light
In the first, spinning place, the spellbound horses walking warm
    Out of the whinnying green stable
        On to the fields of praise.

And honoured among foxes and pheasants by the gay house
Under the new made clouds and happy as the heart was long,
    In the sun born over and over,
        I ran my heedless ways,
    My wishes raced through the house high hay
And nothing I cared, at my sky blue trades, that time allows
In all his tuneful turning so few and such morning songs
    Before the children green and golden
        Follow him out of grace,

Nothing I cared, in the lamb white days, that time would take me
Up to the swallow thronged loft by the shadow of my hand,
    In the moon that is always rising,
        Nor that riding to sleep
    I should hear him fly with the high fields
And wake to the farm forever fled from the childless land.
Oh as I was young and easy in the mercy of his means,
        Time held me green and dying
    Though I sang in my chains like the sea.

Dylan Thomas

Forgotten Language

Once I spoke the language of the flowers,
Once I understood each word the caterpillar said,
Once I smiled in secret at the gossip of the starlings,
And shared a conversation with the housefly
      in my bed.
Once I heard and answered all the questions
      of the crickets,
And joined the crying of each falling dying
      flake of snow,
Once I spoke the language of the flowers. . . .
      How did it go?
      How did it go?

Shel Silverstein

Young Apple Tree, December

for Florence Ladd

What you want for it is what you'd want
for a child: that she take hold;
that her roots find home in stony

winter soil; that she take seasons
in stride, seasons that shape and
reshape her; that like a dancer's,

her limbs grow pliant, graceful
and surprising; that she know,
in her branchings, to seek balance;

that she know when to flower, when
to wait for the returns; that she turn
to a giving sun; that she know to share

fruit as it ripens, that what's lost
to her will be replaced; that early
summer afternoons, a full blossoming

tree, she cast lacy shadows; that change
not frighten her, rather change
meet her embrace; that remembering

her small history, she find her place
in an orchard; that she be her own
orchard; that she outlast you;

that she prepare for the hungry world,
the fallen world, the loony world,
something shapely, useful, new delicious.

Gail Mazur

In the Tree House

I empty the rusty teapot
of blue water, mud and leaves,
retrieve pink tea cups
from the sand box, plastic food
strewn through the woods.
I put cups back on their hooks,
arrange ham beside pepper,
cabbage and egg.
I would live here forever

but as I sweep
sand from the burners
on the painted toy stove,
sand my six year-old calls fire—
why can't you just leave it?—
I remember this house is hers,
and I have to give it back, leave
a little fire on the stove,
the sink, fire even on the floor.

Amy Dryansky

The Barefoot Boy

(excerpt)

All the world I saw or knew
Seemed a complex Chinese toy
Fashioned for a barefoot boy!
Oh, for festal dainties spread,
Like my bowl of milk and bread,
Pewter spoon and bowl of wood,
On the doorstone, gray and rude!
O'er me, like a regal tent,
Cloudy-ribbed, the sunset bent,
Purple-curtained, fringed with gold,
Looped in many a wind-swung fold.
While for music came the play
Of the pied frogs' orchestra,
And, to light the noisy choir,
Lit the fly his lamp of fire.
I was monarch: pomp and joy
Waited on thee, barefoot boy!

John Greenleaf Whittier

Four Haiku

a gathering of stars—
children, grandchildren
great-great-grandchildren

which of you owns
that red moon
children?

an uproar on the beach—
children
and plovers

tickling the baby
in the basket awake . . .
little butterfly

Issa

Translated from the Japanese
by David G. Lanoue

I have a daughter

(poem fragment)

I have a daughter   shaped

like a golden bouquet   I wouldn't

give up   my darling Kleis

for Lydia   all of it

or even   lovely . . .

Sappho

Translated from the ancient Greek
by Robert Bagg

Pine Forest

Let us go now into the forest.
Trees will pass by your face,
and I will stop and offer you to them,
but they cannot bend down.
The night watches over its creatures,
except for the pine trees that never change:
the old wounded springs that spring
blessed gum, eternal afternoons.
If they could, the trees would lift you
and carry you from valley to valley,
and you would pass from arm to arm,
a child running
from father to father.

Gabriela Mistral

Translated from the Spanish
by Maria Giachetti

Remember

Remember the sky that you were born under,
know each of the star's stories.
Remember the moon, know who she is.
Remember the sun's birth at dawn, that is the
strongest point of time. Remember sundown
and the giving away to night.
Remember your birth, how your mother struggled
to give you form and breath. You are evidence of her life, and her
        mother's, and hers.
Remember your father. He is your life, also.
Remember the earth whose skin you are:
red earth, black earth, yellow earth, white earth
brown earth, we are earth.
Remember the plants, trees, animal life who all have their
tribes, their families, their histories, too. Talk to them,
listen to them. They are alive poems.
Remember the wind. Remember her voice. She knows the
origin of this universe.
Remember you are all people and all people are you.
Remember you are this universe and this
universe is you.
Remember all is in motion, is growing, is you.
Remember language comes from this.
Remember the dance language is, that life is.
Remember.

Joy Harjo

Some Questions You Might Ask

Is the soul solid, like iron?
Or is it tender and breakable, like
the wings of a moth in the beak of the owl?
Who has it, and who doesn't?
I keep looking around me.
The face of the moose is as sad
as the face of Jesus.
The swan opens her white wings slowly.
In the fall, the black bear carries leaves into the darkness.
One question leads to another.
Does it have a shape? Like an iceberg?
Like the eye of a hummingbird?
Does it have one lung, like the snake and the scallop?
Why should I have it, and not the anteater
who loves her children?
Why should I have it, and not the camel?
Come to think of it, what about the maple trees?
What about the blue iris?
What about all the little stones, sitting alone in the moonlight?
What about roses, and lemons, and their shining leaves?
What about the grass?

Mary Oliver

It Is a Beauteous Evening, Calm and Free

It is a beauteous evening, calm and free;
The holy time is quiet as a Nun
Breathless with adoration; the broad sun
Is sinking down in its tranquility;
The gentleness of heaven broods o'er the Sea:
Listen! the mighty Being is awake,
And doth with his eternal motion make
A sound like thunder—everlastingly.
Dear child! dear girl! that walkest with me here,
If thou appear untouched by solemn thought,
Thy nature is not therefore less divine:
Thou liest in Abraham's bosom all the year;
And worship'st at the Temple's inner shrine,
God being with thee when we know it not.

William Wordsworth

IX

Lessons

To that high, far-off, favorite place

Where you may stretch and watch and sing

—"Wisdom and Stature,"
Mary Priscilla Howes

You Begin

You begin this way:
this is your hand,
this is your eye,
that is a fish, blue and flat
on the paper, almost
the shape of an eye.
This is your mouth, this is an O
or a moon, whichever
you like. This is yellow.

Outside the window
is the rain, green
because it is summer, and beyond that
the trees and then the world,
which is round and has only
the colors of these nine crayons.

This is the world, which is fuller
and more difficult to learn than I have said.
You are right to smudge it that way
with the red and then
the orange: the world burns.

Once you have learned these words
you will learn that there are more
words than you can ever learn.
The word *hand* floats above your hand
like a small cloud over a lake.
The word *hand* anchors
your hand to this table,

your hand is a warm stone
I hold between two words.

This is your hand, these are my hands, this is the world,
which is round but not flat and has more colors
than we can see.

It begins, it has an end,
this is what you will
come back to, this is your hand.

Margaret Atwood

Wisdom and Stature

Son, I would hold you close,
But no!
Best that I let you go.
I watch you start for the hill-top high,
One hand holding a glass for spying,
In your pocket another for magnifying.
You climb to silence and sun and space,
To that high, far-off, favorite place
Where you may stretch and watch and sing,
Ask questions,—then hide every trace
Of even wondering
About the large, the small,
What matters much, what not at all.
Though I would rather hold you close
And tell you things I've come to know,
Best that I let you go.
Yes go, small son,
And grow!

Mary Priscilla Howes

Growing Up

When I grow up,
I want to be a doctor.

M'ija, you will patch scraped knees
and wipe away children's tears.

But what if I become an architect?

M'ija, you will build beautiful houses
where children will sing and play.

And what if I become a teacher?

M'ija, you will teach
your students to read every day.

But what if I become a famous chef?

M'ija, your arroz con pollo
will be eaten with gozo.

And Mami, what if I want to be like you someday?

M'ija, why do you want to be like me?

Oh Mami, because you care for people, our house is built on love,
you are wise, and your spicy stew tastes delicious.

Liz Ann Báez Aguilar

M'ija (MEE-hah): affectionate form of "mi hija," which means "my daughter"
arroz con pollo (ah-RROHS KOHN POH-yoh): rice with chicken
gozo (GOH-soh): pleasure

I Stop Writing the Poem

to fold the clothes. No matter who lives
or who dies, I'm still a woman.
I'll always have plenty to do.
I bring the arms of his shirt
together. Nothing can stop
our tenderness. I'll get back
to the poem. I'll get back to being
a woman. But for now
there's a shirt, a giant shirt
in my hands, and somewhere a small girl
standing next to her mother
watching to see how it's done.

Tess Gallagher

Advice to a Girl

No one worth possessing
Can be quite possessed;
Lay that on your heart,
My young angry dear;
This truth, this hard and precious stone,
Lay it on your hot cheek,
Let it hide your tear.
Hold it like a crystal
When you are alone
And gaze in the depths of the icy stone.
Long, look long and you will be blessed:
No one worth possessing
Can be quite possessed.

Sara Teasdale

Mythmaker

We lived by the words
of gods, mythologies

you'd mold our history to.
How many nights, you,

a young father, squint-eyed
from books and lamplight,

weaving lessons into bedtime—
the story of Icarus wanting

to soar, (like me on my swing set)
not heeding a father's words,

his fall likened to mine.
I'd carry his doom to sleep,

and that of Narcissus too,
his watered face floating

beautiful and tragic above
my head. My own face

a mirrored comfort
you'd pull me from. Late,

when my dreams turned
to nightmare, you were there—

Beowulf to slay Grendel
at my door. The blood on your hands

you'd anoint my head with.
You would have me bold, fearless—

these were things you needed
to teach me. Warning and wisdom.

You couldn't have known
how I'd take your words and shape

them in creation, reinvent you
a thousand times, making you

forever young and invincible.
Not like now. Not like now.

Natasha Trethewey

Eternity

He who binds to himself a joy
Does the winged life destroy;
But he who kisses the joy as it flies
Lives in eternity's sun rise.

William Blake

A Barred Owl

The warping night air having brought the boom
Of an owl's voice into her darkened room,
We tell the wakened child that all she heard
Was an odd question from a forest bird,
Asking of us, if rightly listened to,
"Who cooks for you?" and then "Who cooks for you?"

Words, which can make our terrors bravely clear,
Can also thus domesticate a fear,
And send a small child back to sleep at night
Not listening for the sound of stealthy flight
Or dreaming of some small thing in a claw
Borne up to some dark branch and eaten raw.

Richard Wilbur

We Started Home, My Son and I

We started home, my son and I.
Twilight already. The young moon
stood in the western sky and beside it
a single star. I showed them to my son
and explained how the moon should be greeted
and that this star is the moon's servant.
As we neared home, he said
that the moon is far, as far
as that place where we went.
I told him the moon is much, much farther
and reckoned: if one were to walk
ten kilometers each day, it would take
almost a hundred years to reach the moon.
But this was not what he wanted to hear.
The road was already almost dry.
The river was spread on the marsh; ducks and other waterfowl
crowed the beginning of night. The snow's crust
crackled underfoot—it must
have been freezing again. All the houses' windows
were dark. Only in our kitchen
a light shone. Beside our chimney, the shining moon,
and beside the moon, a single star.

Jaan Kaplinski

*Translated from the Estonian
by Jaan Kaplinski with
Sam Hamill and
Riina Tamm*

Full Moon and Little Frieda

A cool small evening shrunk to a dog bark and the clank of a bucket—

And you listening.
A spider's web, tense for the dew's touch.
A pail lifted, still and brimming—mirror
To tempt a first star to a tremor.

Cows are going home in the lane there, looping the hedges with their
    warm wreaths of breath—
A dark river of blood, many boulders,
Balancing unspilled milk.

"Moon!" you cry suddenly, "Moon! Moon!"

The moon has stepped back like an artist gazing amazed at a work

That points at him amazed.

Ted Hughes

After Making Love We Hear Footsteps

For I can snore like a bullhorn
or play loud music
or sit up talking with any reasonably sober Irishman
and Fergus will only sink deeper
into his dreamless sleep, which goes by all in one flash,
but let there be that heavy breathing
or a stifled come-cry anywhere in the house
and he will wrench himself awake
and make for it on the run—as now, we lie together,
after making love, quiet, touching along the length of our bodies,
familiar touch of the long-married,
and he appears—in his baseball pajamas, it happens,
the neck opening so small he has to screw them on—
and flops down between us and hugs us and snuggles himself to sleep,
his face gleaming with satisfaction at being this very child.

In the half darkness we look at each other
and smile
and touch arms across this little, startlingly muscled body—
this one whom habit of memory propels to the ground of his making,
sleeper only the mortal sounds can sing awake,
this blessing love gives again into our arms.

Galway Kinnell

Leisure

What is this life if, full of care,
We have no time to stand and stare?—

No time to stand beneath the boughs,
And stare as long as sheep and cows:

No time to see, when woods we pass,
Where squirrels hide their nuts in grass:

No time to see, in broad daylight,
Streams full of stars, like skies at night:

No time to turn at Beauty's glance,
And watch her feet, how they can dance:

No time to wait till her mouth can
Enrich that smile her eyes began?

A poor life this if, full of care,
We have no time to stand and stare.

W. H. Davies

Blackberries for Amelia

Fringing the woods, the stone walls, and the lanes,
Old thickets everywhere have come alive,
Their new leaves reaching out in fans of five
From tangles overarched by this year's canes.

They have their flowers too, it being June,
And here or there in brambled dark-and-light
Are small, five-petaled blooms of chalky white,
As random-clustered and as loosely strewn

As the far stars, of which we now are told
That ever faster do they bolt away,
And that a night may come in which, some say,
We shall have only blackness to behold.

I have no time for any change so great,
But I shall see the August weather spur
Berries to ripen where the flowers were—
Dark berries, savage-sweet and worth the wait—

And there will come the moment to be quick
And save some from the birds, and I shall need
Two pails, old clothes in which to stain and bleed,
And a grandchild to talk with while we pick.

Richard Wilbur

What sort of grandmother

when water and sky are swollen, gunmetal gray
and the egret wading in the marsh is a white that makes
everything else in the world recede, and the slightest
motion of oar, trailing hand, or leaf creates a wake
that might circle the globe and return to lap
this particular silence as heat transforms
to needle the sky with lightning, and day
plays starless night,

takes the child,
yes, with a lifejacket, in the kayak
and shows her the wild peace of the world?

And who's to say which is fossil
and which is living creature leaving its mark?

Rebecca Okrent

Knowledge

It wasn't as if we knew nothing before.
After all, colored girls must know many
things in order to survive. Not only
could I sew buttons and hems, but I could
make a dress and pantaloons from scratch.
I could milk cows, churn butter, feed chickens,
clean their coops, wring their necks, pluck and cook them.
I cut wood, set fires, and boiled water
to wash the clothes and sheets, then wrung them dry.
And I could read the Bible. Evenings
before the fire, my family tired
from unending work and New England cold,
they'd close their eyes. My favorite was Song of Songs.
They most liked when I read, "In the beginning."

Elizabeth Alexander

X
Wisdom and Courage

Hearts are not had as a gift but hearts are earned

—"A Prayer for My Daughter,"
William Butler Yeats

Manners

For a Child of 1918

My grandfather said to me
as we sat on the wagon seat,
"Be sure to remember to always
speak to everyone you meet."

We met a stranger on foot.
My grandfather's whip tapped his hat.
"Good day, sir. Good day. A fine day."
And I said it and bowed where I sat.

Then we overtook a boy we knew
with his big pet crow on his shoulder.
"Always offer everyone a ride;
don't forget that when you get older,"

my grandfather said. So Willy
climbed up with us, but the crow
gave a "Caw!" and flew off. I was worried.
How would he know where to go?

But he flew a little way at a time
from fence post to fence post, ahead;
and when Willy whistled he answered.
"A fine bird," my grandfather said,

"and he's well brought up. See, he answers
nicely when he's spoken to.
Man or beast, that's good manners.
Be sure that you both always do."

When automobiles went by,
the dust hid the people's faces,
but we shouted "Good day! Good day!
Fine day!" at the top of our voices.

When we came to Hustler Hill,
he said that the mare was tired,
so we all got down and walked,
as our good manners required.

Elizabeth Bishop

A Prayer for My Daughter

Once more the storm is howling, and half hid
Under this cradle-hood and coverlid
My child sleeps on. There is no obstacle
But Gregory's wood and one bare hill
Whereby the haystack- and roof-levelling wind,
Bred on the Atlantic, can be stayed;
And for an hour I have walked and prayed
Because of the great gloom that is in my mind.

I have walked and prayed for this young child an hour
And heard the sea-wind scream upon the tower,
And under the arches of the bridge, and scream
In the elms above the flooded stream;
Imagining in excited reverie
That the future years had come,
Dancing to a frenzied drum,
Out of the murderous innocence of the sea.

May she be granted beauty and yet not
Beauty to make a stranger's eye distraught,
Or hers before a looking-glass, for such,
Being made beautiful overmuch,
Consider beauty a sufficient end,
Lose natural kindness and maybe
The heart-revealing intimacy
That chooses right, and never find a friend.

Helen being chosen found life flat and dull
And later had much trouble from a fool,
While that great Queen, that rose out of the spray,
Being fatherless could have her way

Yet chose a bandy-leggèd smith for man.
It's certain that fine women eat
A crazy salad with their meat
Whereby the Horn of Plenty is undone.

In courtesy I'd have her chiefly learned;
Hearts are not had as a gift but hearts are earned
By those that are not entirely beautiful;
Yet many, that have played the fool
For beauty's very self, has charm made wise,
And many a poor man that has roved,
Loved and thought himself beloved,
From a glad kindness cannot take his eyes.

May she become a flourishing hidden tree
That all her thoughts may like the linnet be,
And have no business but dispensing round
Their magnanimities of sound,
Nor but in merriment begin a chase,
Nor but in merriment a quarrel.
O may she live like some green laurel
Rooted in one dear perpetual place.

My mind, because the minds that I have loved,
The sort of beauty that I have approved,
Prosper but little, has dried up of late,
Yet knows that to be choked with hate
May well be of all evil chances chief.
If there's no hatred in a mind
Assault and battery of the wind
Can never tear the linnet from the leaf.

An intellectual hatred is the worst,
So let her think opinions are accursed.
Have I not seen the loveliest woman born
Out of the mouth of Plenty's horn,
Because of her opinionated mind
Barter that horn and every good
By quiet natures understood
For an old bellows full of angry wind?

Considering that, all hatred driven hence,
The soul recovers radical innocence
And learns at last that it is self-delighting,
Self-appeasing, self-affrighting,
And that its own sweet will is Heaven's will;
She can, though every face should scowl
And every windy quarter howl
Or every bellows burst, be happy still.

And may her bridegroom bring her to a house
Where all's accustomed, ceremonious;
For arrogance and hatred are the wares
Peddled in the thoroughfares.
How but in custom and in ceremony
Are innocence and beauty born?
Ceremony's a name for the rich horn,
And custom for the spreading laurel tree.

William Butler Yeats

If

If you can keep your head when all about you
Are losing theirs and blaming it on you;
If you can trust yourself when all men doubt you,
But make allowance for their doubting too:
If you can wait and not be tired by waiting,
Or, being lied about, don't deal in lies,
Or being hated don't give way to hating,
And yet don't look too good, nor talk too wise;

If you can dream—and not make dreams your master;
If you can think—and not make thoughts your aim,
If you can meet with Triumph and Disaster
And treat those two impostors just the same:
If you can bear to hear the truth you've spoken
Twisted by knaves to make a trap for fools,
Or watch the things you gave your life to, broken,
And stoop and build 'em up with worn-out tools;

If you can make one heap of all your winnings
And risk it on one turn of pitch-and-toss,
And lose, and start again at your beginnings,
And never breathe a word about your loss:
If you can force your heart and nerve and sinew
To serve your turn long after they are gone,
And so hold on when there is nothing in you
Except the Will which says to them: "Hold on!"

If you can talk with crowds and keep your virtue,
Or walk with Kings—nor lose the common touch,
If neither foes nor loving friends can hurt you,
If all men count with you, but none too much:

If you can fill the unforgiving minute
With sixty seconds' worth of distance run,
Yours is the Earth and everything that's in it,
And—which is more—you'll be a Man, my son!

Rudyard Kipling

Nobility

True worth is in *being*, not *seeming*,—
    In doing, each day that goes by,
Some little good—not in dreaming
    Of great things to do by and by.
For whatever men say in their blindness,
    And spite of the fancies of youth,
There's nothing so kingly as kindness,
    And nothing so royal as truth.

We get back our mete as we measure—
    We cannot do wrong and feel right,
Nor can we give pain and gain pleasure,
    For justice avenges each slight.
The air for the wing of the sparrow,
    The bush for the robin and wren,
But always the path that is narrow
    And straight, for the children of men.

'Tis not in the pages of story
    The heart of its ills to beguile,
Though he who makes courtship to glory
    Gives all that he hath for her smile.
For when from her heights he has won her,
    Alas! it is only to prove
That nothing's so sacred as honor,
    And nothing so loyal as love!

We cannot make bargains for blisses,
    Nor catch them like fishes in nets;
And sometimes the thing our life misses
    Helps more than the thing which it gets.

For good lieth not in pursuing,
     Nor gaining of great nor of small,
But just in the doing, and doing
     As we would be done by, is all.

Through envy, through malice, through hating,
     Against the world, early and late,
No jot of our courage abating—
     Our part is to work and to wait.
And slight is the sting of his trouble
     Whose winnings are less than his worth;
For he who is honest is noble,
     Whatever his fortunes or birth.

Alice Cary

The Red Hat

It started before Christmas. Now our son
officially walks to school alone.
Semi-alone, it's accurate to say:
I or his father track him on the way.
He walks up on the east side of West End,
we on the west side. Glances can extend
(and do) across the street; not eye contact.
Already ties are feeling and not fact.
Straus Park is where these parallel paths part;
he goes alone from there. The watcher's heart
stretches, elastic in its love and fear,
toward him as we see him disappear,
striding briskly. Where two weeks ago,
holding a hand, he'd dawdle, dreamy, slow,
he now is hustled forward by the pull
of something far more powerful than school.

The mornings we turn back to are no more
than forty minutes longer than before,
but they feel vastly different—flimsy, strange,
wavering in the eddies of this change,
empty, unanchored, perilously light
since the red hat vanished from our sight.

Rachel Hadas

The Beatitudes

Blessed are the poor in spirit: for theirs is the kingdom of heaven.

Blessed are they that mourn: for they shall be comforted.

Blessed are the meek: for they shall inherit the earth.

Blessed are they which do hunger and thirst after righteousness: for they shall be filled.

Blessed are the merciful: for they shall obtain mercy.

Blessed are the pure in heart: for they shall see God.

Blessed are the peacemakers: for they shall be called the children of God.

Blessed are they which are persecuted for righteousness' sake: for theirs is the kingdom of heaven.

> The Gospel According to Saint Matthew, 5:2–10
> The Bible, King James Version

Gifts for my girl

to my youngest daughter, Kristin

At eleven, you need new shoes
often, and I would give you
other things to stand on
that are handsome and useful
and fit you well, that are not
all plastic, that are real
and knowable and leather-
hard, things that will move
with you and breathe rain
or air, and wear
well in all weather.

For beauty, I would buy
a gem for you from the earth's
heart and a ring that is gold
clear through and clothes the colors
of flowers. I would cultivate in you
a gentle spirit, and curiosity,
and wonder in your eyes. For use,
in your house I'd hang
doors that are solid wood
without hidden panels of air, set
in walls built of brick more
then one inch thick.
On your floors I'd stretch fleeces
from black sheep's backs
and for your sleep, sheets
spun from fibers that grew, once,
on the flanks of the fields.
I'd mount for you one small,

clean mirror for a grinning
glimpse at yourself, and a whole
geometry of windows to the world,
with sashes that open hard, but
once lifted, let in a breath
of pure sun, the smell of a day,
a taste of wild wind, an earful
of green music.

At eleven, and always,
you will need to be nourished.
For your mind—poems and plays, words
on the pages of a thousand books:
Deuteronomy, Dante and Donne,
Hosea and Hopkins, L'Engle and Lewis.
For your spirit, mysteries and praise,
sureties and prayer. For your teeth
and tongue, real bread the color
of grain at a feast, baked and broken
fresh each day, apricots and raisins,
cheese and olive oil and honey
that live bees have brought
from the orchard. For drink
I'd pour you a wine
that remembers sun and shadow
on the hillside where it grew,
and spring water wet enough
to slake your forever thirst.

At eleven, the air around you
is full of calls and strange
directions. Choices pull at you
and a confusion of dreams.

And I would show you a true compass
and how to use it, and a sun steady
in its orbit and a way
through the woods by a path
that will not peter out.

At eleven you know well
the sound of love's voice
and you have, already, hands
and a heart and a mouth
that can answer. And I
would learn with you
more of how love gives and receives,
both, with both palms open. I
am standing here, far enough away
for you to stretch and breathe,
close enough to shield you from
some of the chill and to tell you
of a comfort that is
stronger, more real,
that will come closer still.

Luci Shaw

For the Record

His right hand holds his slingshot,
His left a clay pellet.
He sits there, back against a pillar,
His legs straight, watching the sky
With his black eyes,
Stalking the crows that come
To steal the grapes from the arbor.
He intends to kill, but he cannot
Change his expression—filled with affection.
When I suddenly caught sight of him
From the window,
My eyes filled with tears.

Ping Hsin

*Translated from the Chinese
by Kenneth Rexroth and Ling Chung*

What Are Heavy?

What are heavy? sea-sand and sorrow:
What are brief? today and tomorrow:
What are frail? Spring blossoms and youth:
What are deep? the ocean and truth.

Christina Rossetti

My Three-year-old Son Hears of Death from a Neighbor

The brat next door has told you all of us will die.
I'm unprepared.
Want to shout: Not so! Never me. Not you.
You're full of tears.
Both of us wounded by the news
and I, unwilling to describe a paradise
you'd have to die to know.

Come to the window.
See the starlight dancing on the snowy field?

If you were dying I would make you a heaven
your friends would envy. But I won't
dazzle you with angels who might lift you
out of fear. Away from me.
That brat abused your tenderness, but didn't lie.
Death is true
as the rush of the pasture stream in springtime
weaving gold through the field.

There's heaven for you, where
any god you want is yours.
Choose one who will bend you
in reverence not remorse.

We will become light.

Rebecca Okrent

The Ball Poem

What is the boy now, who has lost his ball,
What what is he to do? I saw it go
Merrily bouncing, down the street, and then
Merrily over—there it is in the water!
No use to say "O there are other balls":
An ultimate shaking grief fixes the boy
As he stands rigid, trembling, staring down
All his young days into the harbour where
His ball went. I would not intrude on him,
A dime, another ball, is worthless. Now
He senses first his responsibility
In a world of possessions. People will take balls,
Balls will be lost always, little boy,
And no one buys a ball back. Money is external.
He is learning, far behind his desperate eyes,
The epistemology of loss, how to stand up.
Knowing what every man must one day know
And most know many days, how to stand up.
And gradually light returns to the street,
A whistle blows, the ball is out of sight,
Soon part of me will explore the deep and dark
Floor of the harbour. I am everywhere,
I suffer and move, my mind and my heart move
With all that move me, under the water
Or whistling, I am not a little boy.

John Berryman

Egg

I'm scrambling an egg for my daughter.
"Why are you always whistling?" she asks.
"Because I'm happy."
And it's true,
Though it stuns me to say it aloud,
There was a time when I wouldn't
Have seen it as my future.
It's partly a matter
Of who is there to eat the egg:
The self fallen out of love with itself
Through the tedium of familiarity,
Or this little self,
So curious, so hungry,
Who emerged from the woman I love,
A woman who loves me in a way
I've come to think I deserve,
Now that it arrives from outside me.
Everything changes, we're told,
And now the changes are everywhere:
The house with its morning light
That fills me like a revelation,
The yard with its trees
That cast a bit more shade each summer,
The love of a woman
That both is and isn't confounding,
And the love
Of this clamor of questions at my waist.
Clamor of questions,
You clamor of answers,
Here's your egg.

C. G. Hanzlicek

Peaches

Jenny, because you are twenty-three,
                              (and my daughter,)
you think you know everything;
and because I am fifty-three,
                              (and your mother,)
I think *I* know everything.
A week ago you picked up two green little peaches,
hard and half-grown,
from under the loaded peach tree
and put them on the kitchen window sill;
and I thought
                    (though I didn't say a word:)
they're too small, they will just rot
but I won't move them—
                              Jenny put them there.
Now the summer is over and you are gone,
the mornings are cool, the squash conquers the garden,
the tree swallows have flown, crickets begin to sing—
and the sweet juice of your peaches runs down my chin.

                                        Kate Barnes

What I Learned from My Mother

I learned from my mother how to love
the living, to have plenty of vases on hand
in case you have to rush to the hospital
with peonies cut from the lawn, black ants
still stuck to the buds. I learned to save jars
large enough to hold fruit salad for a whole
grieving household, to cube home-canned pears
and peaches, to slice through maroon grape skins
and flick out the sexual seeds with a knife point.
I learned to attend viewings even if I didn't know
the deceased, to press the moist hands
of the living, to look in their eyes and offer
sympathy, as though I understood loss even then.
I learned that whatever we say means nothing,
what anyone will remember is that we came.
I learned to believe I had the power to ease
awful pains materially like an angel.
Like a doctor, I learned to create
from another's suffering my own usefulness, and once
you know how to do this, you can never refuse.
To every house you enter, you must offer
healing: a chocolate cake you baked yourself,
the blessing of your voice, your chaste touch.

Julia Kasdorf

XI
Of Night and Light and Half-Light

I wish

What I wished you before, but harder

—"The Writer,"
Richard Wilbur

The Writer

In her room at the prow of the house
Where light breaks, and the windows are tossed with linden,
My daughter is writing a story.

I pause in the stairwell, hearing
From her shut door a commotion of typewriter-keys
Like a chain hauled over a gunwale.

Young as she is, the stuff
Of her life is a great cargo, and some of it heavy:
I wish her a lucky passage.

But now it is she who pauses,
As if to reject my thought and its easy figure.
A stillness greatens, in which

The whole house seems to be thinking,
And then she is at it again with a bunched clamor
Of strokes, and again is silent.

I remember the dazed starling
Which was trapped in that very room, two years ago;
How we stole in, lifted a sash

And retreated, not to affright it;
And how for a helpless hour, through the crack of the door,
We watched the sleek, wild, dark

And iridescent creature
Batter against the brilliance, drop like a glove
To the hard floor, or the desk-top,

And wait then, humped and bloody,
For the wits to try it again; and how our spirits
Rose when, suddenly sure,

It lifted off from a chair-back,
Beating a smooth course for the right window
And clearing the sill of the world.

It is always a matter, my darling,
Of life or death, as I had forgotten. I wish
What I wished you before, but harder.

Richard Wilbur

He Wishes for the Cloths of Heaven

Had I the heavens' embroidered cloths,
Enwrought with golden and silver light,
The blue and the dim and the dark cloths
Of night and light and half-light,
I would spread the cloths under your feet:
But I, being poor, have only my dreams;
I have spread my dreams under your feet;
Tread softly because you tread on my dreams.

William Butler Yeats

Perseverance

We must not hope to be mowers,
    And to gather the ripe gold ears,
Unless we have first been sowers
    And watered the furrows with tears.

It is not just as we take it,
    This mystical world of ours,
Life's field will yield as we make it
    A harvest of thorns or of flowers.

        Johann Wolfgang von Goethe
        Translated from the German
        by Alice Cary

Reading the Brothers Grimm to Jenny

Jenny, your mind commands
kingdoms of black and white:
you shoulder the crow on your left,
the snowbird on your right;
for you the cinders part
and let the lentils through,
and noise falls into place
as screech or sweet roo-coo,
while in my own real world
gray foxes and gray wolves
bargain eye to eye,
and the amazing dove
takes shelter under the wing
of the raven to keep dry.

Knowing that you must climb,
one day, the ancient tower
where disenchantment binds
the curls of innocence,
that you must live with power
and honor circumstance,
that choice is what comes true—
O, Jenny, pure in heart,
why do I lie to you?

Why do I read you tales
in which birds speak the truth
and pity cures the blind,
and beauty reaches deep
to prove a royal mind?
Death is a small mistake

there, where the kiss revives;
Jenny, we make just dreams
out of our unjust lives.

Still, when your truthful eyes,
your keen, attentive stare,
endow the vacuous slut
with royalty, when you match
her soul to her shimmering hair,
what can she do but rise
to your imagined throne?
And what can I, but see
beyond the world that is,
when, faithful, you insist
I have the golden key—
and learn from you once more
the terror and the bliss,
the world as it might be?

                    Lisel Mueller

After Work

Coming up from the subway
into the cool Manhattan evening,
I feel rough hands on my heart—
women in the market yelling
over rows of tomatoes and peppers,
old men sitting on a stoop playing cards,
cabbies cursing each other with fists
while the music of church bells
sails over the street,
and the father, angry and tired
after working all day,
embracing his little girl,
kissing her,
mi vida, mi corazón,
brushing the hair out of her eyes
so she can see.

Richard Jones

Prayer for My Children

I regret nothing.
My cruelties, my betrayals
of others I once thought
I loved. All the unlived
years, the unwritten
poems, the wasted nights
spent weeping and drinking.

No, I regret nothing
because what I've lived
has led me here, to this room
with its marvelous riches
its simple wealth—
these three heads shining
beneath the Japanese lamp, laboring
over crayons and paper.
These three who love me
exactly as I am, precisely
at the center of my ill-built being.
Who rear up eagerly when I enter,
and fall down weeping when I leave.
Whose eyes are my eyes
Hair, my hair.
Whose bodies I cover
with kisses and blankets.
Whose first meal was my own body.
Whose last, please God, I will not live
To serve, or share.

Kate Daniels

There Was a Child Went Forth

There was a child went forth every day;
And the first object he look'd upon, that object he became;
And that object became part of him for the day, or a certain part of the
day, or for many years, or stretching cycles of years.

The early lilacs became part of this child,
And grass, and white and red morning-glories, and white and red
clover, and the song of the phoebe-bird,
And the Third-month lambs, and the sow's pink-faint litter, and the
mare's foal, and the cow's calf,
And the noisy brood of the barn-yard, or by the mire of the pond-
side,
And the fish suspending themselves so curiously below there—and
the beautiful curious liquid,
And the water-plants with their graceful flat heads—all became part
of him.

The field-sprouts of Fourth-month and Fifth-month became part of
him;
Winter-grain sprouts, and those of the light-yellow corn, and the
esculent roots of the garden,
And the apple-trees cover'd with blossoms, and the fruit afterward,
and wood-berries, and the commonest weeds by the road;
And the old drunkard staggering home from the out-house of the
tavern, whence he had lately risen,
And the school-mistress that pass'd on her way to the school,
And the friendly boys that pass'd—and the quarrelsome boys,
And the tidy and fresh-cheek'd girls—and the barefoot negro boy and
girl,
And all the changes of city and country, wherever he went.

His own parents,

He that had father'd him, and she that had conceiv'd him in her
womb, and birth'd him,

They gave this child more of themselves than that;

They gave him afterward every day—they became part of him.

The mother at home, quietly placing the dishes on the supper-table;

The mother with mild words—clean her cap and gown, a wholesome
odor falling off her person and clothes as she walks by;

The father, strong, self-sufficient, manly, mean, anger'd, unjust;

The blow, the quick loud word, the tight bargain, the crafty lure,

The family usages, the language, the company, the furniture—the
yearning and swelling heart,

Affection that will not be gainsay'd—the sense of what is real—the
thought if, after all, it should prove unreal,

The doubts of day-time and the doubts of night-time—the curious
whether and how,

Whether that which appears so is so, or is it all flashes and specks?

Men and women crowding fast in the streets—if they are not flashes
and specks, what are they?

The streets themselves, and the façades of houses, and goods in the
windows,

Vehicles, teams, the heavy-plank'd wharves—the huge crossing at the
ferries,

The village on the highland, seen from afar at sunset—the river between,

Shadows, aureola and mist, the light falling on roofs and gables of
white or brown, three miles off,

The schooner near by, sleepily dropping down the tide—the little boat
slack-tow'd astern,

The hurrying tumbling waves, quick-broken crests, slapping,

The strata of color'd clouds, the long bar of maroon-tint, away solitary
by itself—the spread of purity it lies motionless in,

The horizon's edge, the flying sea-crow, the fragrance of salt marsh
and shore mud;
These became part of that child who went forth every day, and who
now goes, and will always go forth every day.

Walt Whitman

A Blank

The year of griefs being through, they had to merge
In one last grief, with one last property:
To view itself like loosened cloud lose edge,
And pull apart, and leave a voided sky.

Watching Victorian porches through the glass,
From the 6 bus, I caught sight of a friend
Stopped on a corner-kerb to let us pass,
A four-year-old blond child tugging his hand,
Which tug he held against with a slight smile.
I knew the smile from certain passages
Two years ago, thus did not know him well,
Since they took place in my bedroom and his.

A sturdy-looking admirable young man.
He said "I chose to do this with my life."
Casually met he said it of the plan
He undertook without a friend or wife.

Now visibly tugged upon by his decision,
Wayward and eager. So this was his son!
What I admired about his self-permission
Was that he turned from nothing he had done,
Or was, or had been, even while he transposed
The expectations he took out at dark
—Of Eros playing, features undisclosed—
Into another pitch, where he might work

With the same melody, and opted so
To educate, permit, guide, feed, keep warm,

And love a child to be adopted, though
The child was still a blank then on a form.

The blank was flesh now, running on its nerve,
This fair-topped organism dense with charm,
Its braided muscle grabbing what would serve,
His countering pull, his own devoted arm.

                              Thom Gunn

Born Yesterday
for Sally Amis

Tightly-folded bud,
I have wished you something
None of the others would:
Not the usual stuff
About being beautiful,
Or running off a spring
Of innocence and love—
They will all wish you that,
And should it prove possible,
Well, you're a lucky girl.

But if it shouldn't, then
May you be ordinary;
Have, like other women,
An average of talents:
Not ugly, not good-looking,
Nothing uncustomary
To pull you off your balance,
That, unworkable itself,
Stops all the rest from working.
In fact, may you be dull—
If that is what a skilled,
Vigilant, flexible,
Unemphasised, enthralled
Catching of happiness is called.

Philip Larkin

Happiness

I asked the professors who teach the meaning of life to tell
    me what is happiness.
And I went to famous executives who boss the work of
    thousands of men.
They all shook their heads and gave me a smile as though
    I was trying to fool with them.
And then one Sunday afternoon I wandered out along
    the Desplaines river.
And I saw a crowd of Hungarians under the trees with
    their women and children and a keg of beer and an
    accordion.

Carl Sandburg

Nancy Hanks

If Nancy Hanks
Came back as a ghost,
Seeking news
Of what she loved most,
She'd ask first
"Where's my son?
What's happened to Abe?
What's he done?"

"Poor little Abe,
Left all alone
Except for Tom,
Who's a rolling stone;
He was only nine
The year I died.
I remember still
How hard he cried."

"Scraping along
In a little shack,
With hardly a shirt
To cover his back,
And a prairie wind
To blow him down,
Or pinching times
If he went to town."

"You wouldn't know
About my son?
Did he grow tall?
Did he have fun?

Did he learn to read?
Did he get to town?
Do you know his name?
Did he get on?"

Rosemary and
Stephen Vincent Benét

Prayer for a New Mother

The things she knew, let her forget again—
    The voices in the sky, the fear, the cold,
The gaping shepherds, and the queer old men
    Piling their clumsy gifts of foreign gold.

Let her have laughter with her little one;
    Teach her the endless, tuneless songs to sing;
Grant her her right to whisper to her son
    The foolish names one dare not call a king.

Keep from her dreams the rumble of a crowd,
    The smell of rough-cut wood, the trail of red,
The thick and chilly whiteness of the shroud
    That wraps the strange new body of the dead.

Ah, let her go, kind Lord, where mothers go
    And boast his pretty words and ways, and plan
The proud and happy years that they shall know
    Together, when her son is grown a man.

Dorothy Parker

Mother to Son

Well, son, I'll tell you:
Life for me ain't been no crystal stair.
It's had tacks in it,
And splinters,
And boards torn up,
And places with no carpet on the floor—
Bare.
But all the time
I'se been a-climbin' on,
And reachin' landin's,
And turnin' corners,
And sometimes goin' in the dark
Where there ain't been no light.
So boy, don't you turn back.
Don't you set down on the steps
'Cause you finds it's kinder hard.
Don't you fall now—
For I'se still goin' on, honey,
I'se still climbin',
And life for me ain't been no crystal stair.

Langston Hughes

blessing the boats

(at St. Mary's)

may the tide
that is entering even now
the lip of our understanding
carry you out
beyond the face of fear
may you kiss
the wind then turn from it
certain that it will
love you back   may you
open your eyes to water
water waving forever
and may you in your innocence
sail through this to that

Lucille Clifton

XII
Imagination and Memory

Look back on Time with kindly eyes

—"Look Back on Time with Kindly Eyes,"
Emily Dickinson

What Travel Does

My uncle comes home from Siberia
describing the smoked caribou leg
still wearing its hoof
left on the drainboard
week after week,
small knives slicing
sour red flesh.
He becomes a vegetarian.
But he misses the spaciousness.
It wasn't crowded up there.
He ran into a polar bear
the same way you might run into your
mailman around the block.

My teacher returns from China
obsessed by the two-string violin
and the tiny birds in lattice cages.
She plays a tape
as we do our silent reading.

My whole family comes back from Paris
asking why we live anywhere else.
Every interesting person
and tucked neck scarf
looked full of stories.
People paused for peach tarts and crepes
in the middle of the afternoon.

My grandfather comes home
from Palestine
older.

He has been in the camps.
He can't stop aching.

After Mexico, my neighbor Lupe
misses intense color,
won't wear beige anymore.
She prefers papayas sliced
with lime juice drizzled on top.
She feels happy every time she faces south.

Naomi Shihab Nye

The Land of Story-Books

At evening when the lamp is lit,
Around the fire my parents sit;
They sit at home and talk and sing,
And do not play at anything.

Now, with my little gun, I crawl
All in the dark along the wall,
And follow round the forest track
Away behind the sofa back.

There, in the night, where none can spy,
All in my hunter's camp I lie,
And play at books that I have read
Till it is time to go to bed.

These are the hills, these are the woods,
These are my starry solitudes;
And there the river by whose brink
The roaring lions come to drink.

I see the others far away
As if in firelit camp they lay,
And I, like to an Indian scout,
Around their party prowled about.

So when my nurse comes in for me,
Home I return across the sea,
And go to bed with backward looks
At my dear land of Story-books.

Robert Louis Stevenson

To a Daughter Leaving Home

When I taught you
at eight to ride
a bicycle, loping along
beside you
as you wobbled away
on two round wheels,
my own mouth rounding
in surprise when you pulled
ahead down the curved
path of the park,
I kept waiting
for the thud
of your crash as I
sprinted to catch up,
while you grew
smaller, more breakable
with distance,
pumping, pumping
for your life, screaming
with laughter,
the hair flapping
behind you like a
handkerchief waving
goodbye.

Linda Pastan

What Memories Will Rise

Parents are a strange lot, we make
our children's memories like a quilt,
choosing the fabric and the color. We shape
the pattern. As they grow into adults

we hope they'll wear around them as a charm
the heat of ledgy rocks along the coast,
acres of sharp raspberries at the farm,
the bang of a screen door in the summer dusk.

Will they tell their sons and daughters of the taste
of wild blueberries in a pie,
of the night I woke them and we raced
to see Perseid showers in the sky?

Will the scent of lilac bring them back
to their cluttered dressers full of blooms?
Will they hear their skis in frozen tracks
or see the froth of beach plum over dunes?

What memories will rise like slow whales
breaking the opaque surface of their age?
Some boy, we never knew of, who once smiled,
the heartbreak of an empty cage,

the way a face swelled from a sting,
a vision of a car just overturned,
kites lost in trees, birds with broken wings,
how maple leaves shrivel before they burn.

Nightmares, pleasure, passion, they'll forget
the way the ocean ferry soothed their hearts.
What they do remember will be hot,
sweet, bitter, sharp, brilliant as fire sparks.

Judith Steinbergh

Piano

Softly, in the dusk, a woman is singing to me;
Taking me back down the vista of years, till I see
A child sitting under the piano, in the boom of the tingling strings
And pressing the small, poised feet of a mother who smiles as she
    sings.

In spite of myself, the insidious mastery of song
Betrays me back, till the heart of me weeps to belong
To the old Sunday evenings at home, with winter outside
And hymns in the cosy parlour, the tinkling piano our guide.

So now it is vain for the singer to burst into clamour
With the great black piano appassionato. The glamour
Of childish days is upon me, my manhood is cast
Down in the flood of remembrance, I weep like a child for the past.

D. H. Lawrence

Those Winter Sundays

Sundays too my father got up early
and put his clothes on in the blueblack cold,
then with cracked hands that ached
from labor in the weekday weather made
banked fires blaze. No one ever thanked him.

I'd wake and hear the cold splintering, breaking.
When the rooms were warm, he'd call,
and slowly I would rise and dress,
fearing the chronic angers of that house,

Speaking indifferently to him,
who had driven out the cold
and polished my good shoes as well.
What did I know, what did I know
of love's austere and lonely offices?

                              Robert Hayden

Look Back on Time with Kindly Eyes

Look back on Time, with kindly eyes—
He doubtless did his best—
How softly sinks that trembling sun
In Human Nature's West—

                    Emily Dickinson

Green Behind the Ears

I was still slightly
fuzzy in shady spots
and the tenderest lime.
It was lovely, as I
look back, but not
at the time. For it is
hard to be green and
take your turn as flesh.
So much freshness
to unlearn.

Kay Ryan

Ode: Intimations of Immortality from Recollections of Early Childhood

(excerpt)

The Child is Father of the Man;
And I could wish my days to be
Bound each to each by natural piety.

11.

And O, ye Fountains, Meadows, Hills, and Groves,
Forebode not any severing of our loves!
Yet in my heart of hearts I feel your might;
I only have relinquished one delight
To live beneath your more habitual sway.
I love the Brooks which down their channels fret,
Even more than when I tripped lightly as they;
The innocent brightness of a new-born Day
        Is lovely yet;
The Clouds that gather round the setting sun
Do take a sober colouring from an eye
That hath kept watch o'er man's mortality;
Another race hath been, and other palms are won.
Thanks to the human heart by which we live,
Thanks to its tenderness, its joys, and fears,
To me the meanest flower that blows can give
Thoughts that do often lie too deep for tears.

William Wordsworth

After Disappointment

To lie in your child's bed when she is gone
Is calming as anything I know. To fall
Asleep, her books arranged above your head,
Is to admit that you have never been
So tired, so enchanted by the spell
Of your grown body. To feel small instead
Of blocking out the light, to feel alone,
Not knowing what you should or shouldn't feel,
Is to find out, no matter what you've said
About the cramped escapes and obstacles
You plan and face and have to call the world,
That there remain these places, occupied
By children, yours if lucky, like the girl
Who finds you here and lies down by your side.

                                        Mark Jarman

The Foster Child

Weaving a basket of the day, they
who seldom spoke otherwise
talked in bed.

It was not a house for privacy:
two rooms and a sleeping porch;
I on my couch overheard
everything said.

Propped on pillows, he smoked a pipe,
she fingered rosary beads,
between them the basket was finished

and put aside in the methodical way
they did everything:
played cribbage, carted the leaves away.

No ideas hung on the blackberry vine
they wove into the warp of real things,
words for *mice, feathers,* and *wings,*

for the white cat who loved them,
birch trees and wrens.
A few feet from the door

the waves kept lapping.
I'd never been given before
a sense of containment,

and never got it again,
except I can weave it now on my own,
out of the talk and stillness of that home.

Mary Rose O'Reilley

The Lanyard

The other day I was ricocheting slowly
off the pale blue walls of this room,
bouncing from typewriter to piano,
from bookshelf to an envelope lying on the floor,
I found myself in the L section of the dictionary
where my eyes fell upon the word *lanyard*.

No cookie nibbled by a French novelist
could send one more suddenly into the past—
a past where I sat at a workbench at a camp
by a deep Adirondack lake
learning how to braid thin plastic strips
into a lanyard, a gift for my mother.

I had never seen anyone use a lanyard
or wear one, if that's what you did with them,
but that did not keep me from crossing
strand over strand again and again
until I had made a boxy
red and white lanyard for my mother.

She gave me life and milk from her breasts,
and I gave her a lanyard.
She nursed me in many a sickroom,
lifted teaspoons of medicine to my lips,
set cold face-cloths on my forehead,
and then led me out into the airy light

and taught me to walk and swim,
and I, in turn, presented her with a lanyard.
Here are thousands of meals, she said,

and here is clothing and a good education.
And here is your lanyard, I replied,
which I made with a little help from a counselor.

Here is a breathing body and a beating heart,
strong legs, bones and teeth,
and two clear eyes to read the world, she whispered,
and here, I said, is the lanyard I made at camp.
And here, I wish to say to her now,
is a smaller gift—not the archaic truth

that you can never repay your mother,
but the rueful admission that when she took
the two-tone lanyard from my hands,
I was as sure as a boy could be
that this useless, worthless thing I wove
out of boredom would be enough to make us even.

Billy Collins

To My Mother

To-day's your natal day,
　　Sweet flowers I bring;
Mother, accept, I pray
　　My offering.

And may you happy live,
　　And long us bless;
Receiving as you give
　　Great happiness.

Christina Rossetti

This Pleasing Anxious Being

I

In no time you are back where safety was,
Spying upon the lambent table where
Good family faces drink the candlelight
As in a manger scene by de La Tour.
Father has finished carving at the sideboard
And Mother's hand has touched a little bell,
So that, beside her chair, Roberta looms
With serving bowls of yams and succotash.
When will they speak, or stir? They wait for you
To recollect that, while it lived, the past
Was a rushed present, fretful and unsure.
The muffled clash of silverware begins,
With ghosts of gesture, with a laugh retrieved,
And the warm, edgy voices you would hear:
Rest for a moment in that resonance.
But see your small feet kicking under the table,
Fiercely impatient to be off and play.

II

The shadow of whoever took the picture
Reaches like Azrael's across the sand
Toward grown-ups blithe in black and white, encamped
Where surf behind them floods a rocky cove.
They turn with wincing smiles, shielding their eyes
Against the sunlight and the future's glare,
Which notes their bathing caps, their quaint maillots,
The wicker picnic hamper then in style,

And will convict them of mortality.
Two boys, however, do not plead with time,
Distracted as they are by what?—perhaps
A whacking flash of gull-wings overhead—
While off to one side, with his back to us,
A painter, perched before his easel, seeing
The marbled surges come to various ruin,
Seeks out of all those waves to build a wave
That shall in blue summation break forever.

III

Wild, lashing snow, which thumps against the windshield
Like earth tossed down upon a coffin-lid,
Half clogs the wipers, and our Buick yaws
On the black roads of 1928.
Father is driving; Mother, leaning out,
Tracks with her flashlight beam the pavement's edge,
And we must weather hours more of storm
To be in Baltimore for Christmastime.
Of the two children in the back seat, safe
Beneath a lap-robe, soothed by jingling chains
And by their parents' pluck and gaiety,
One is asleep. The other's half-closed eyes
Make out at times the dark hood of the car
Plowing the eddied flakes, and might foresee
The steady chugging of a landing craft
Through morning mist to the bombarded shore,
Or a deft prow that dances through the rocks
In the white water of the Allagash,
Or, in good time, the bedstead at whose foot
The world will swim and flicker and be gone.

Richard Wilbur

Mirror

When the lamb stood up after birth
    his legs shivering with the world's weight
something exploded inside me
    some memory of how love
translates into bodies and new life
    enters the space between sky and land
to begin walking undeniably toward death
    he with his tiny hooves black
against the white curl of his wool
    and in the sweetness of that face
all living wore new meaning—my son
    who burst out of his upbringing
to scatter me like sunlight from a mirror
    until I found part of myself
inside the lambing pen opening
    the small reluctant mouth onto a teat
and another part on a rocking chair
    in our bedroom of eighteen years ago
nursing a future I couldn't see
    as autumn settled its amber
on maples outside the window
    and his tiny fist cast out
invisible guidelines toward manhood

Susie Patlove

Yellow Bowl

If light pours like water
into the kitchen where I sway
with my tired children,

if the rug beneath us
is woven with tough flowers,
and the yellow bowl on the table

rests with the sweet heft
of fruit, the sun-warmed plums,
if my body curves over the babies,

and if I am singing,
then loneliness has lost its shape,
and this quiet is only quiet.

                Rachel Contreni Flynn

Daystar

She wanted a little room for thinking:
but she saw diapers steaming on the line,
a doll slumped behind the door.

So she lugged a chair behind the garage
to sit out the children's naps.

Sometimes there were things to watch—
the pinched armor of a vanished cricket,
a floating maple leaf. Other days
she stared until she was assured
when she closed her eyes
she'd see only her own vivid blood.

She had an hour, at best, before Liza appeared
pouting from the top of the stairs.
And just *what* was mother doing
out back with the field mice? Why,
building a palace. Later
that night when Thomas rolled over and
lurched into her, she would open her eyes
and think of the place that was hers
for an hour—where
she was nothing,
pure nothing, in the middle of the day.

Rita Dove

The Lake Isle of Innisfree

I will arise and go now, and go to Innisfree,
And a small cabin build there, of clay and wattles made:
Nine bean-rows will I have there, a hive for the honeybee,
And live alone in the bee-loud glade.

And I shall have some peace there, for peace comes dropping slow,
Dropping from the veils of the morning to where the cricket sings;
There midnight's all a glimmer, and noon a purple glow,
And evening full of the linnet's wings.

I will arise and go now, for always night and day
I hear lake water lapping with low sounds by the shore;
While I stand on the roadway, or on the pavements grey,
I hear it in the deep heart's core.

William Butler Yeats

XIII

To Arrive Where We Started

ask that your way be long,
full of adventure, full of instruction

—"Ithaka,"
Constantine P. Cavafy

Spring and Fall

To a Young Child

Márgarét, áre you gríeving
Over Goldengrove unleaving?
Leáves, líke the things of man, you
With your fresh thoughts care for, can you?
Áh! ás the heart grows older
It will come to such sights colder
By and by, nor spare a sigh
Though worlds of wanwood leafmeal lie;
And yet you *will* weep and know why.
Now no matter, child, the name:
Sórrow's spríngs áre the same.
Nor mouth had, no nor mind, expressed
What heart heard of, ghost guessed:
It ís the blight man was born for,
It is Margaret you mourn for.

Gerard Manley Hopkins

A Poem for Emily

Small fact and fingers and farthest one from me,
a hand's width and two generations away,
in this still present I am fifty-three.
You are not yet a full day.

When I am sixty-three, when you are ten,
and you are neither closer nor as far,
your arms will fill with what you know by then,
the arithmetic and love we do and are.

When I by blood and luck am eighty-six
and you are someplace else and thirty-three
believing in sex and god and politics
with children who look not at all like me,

sometime I know you will have read them this
so they will know I love them and say so
and love their mother. Child, whatever is
is always or never was. Long ago,

a day I watched awhile beside your bed,
I wrote this down, a thing that might be kept
awhile, to tell you what I would have said
when you were who knows what and I was dead
which is I stood and loved you while you slept.

Miller Williams

Late Fragment

And did you get what
you wanted from this life, even so?
I did.
And what did you want?
To call myself beloved, to feel myself
beloved on the earth.

Raymond Carver

I Corinthians 13

Though I speak with the tongues of men and of angels, and have not
    charity, I am become as sounding brass, or a tinkling cymbal.

And though I have the gift of prophecy, and understand all mysteries,
    and all knowledge; and though I have all faith, so that I could
    remove mountains, and have not charity, I am nothing.

And though I bestow all my goods to feed the poor, and though I give
    my body to be burned, and have not charity, it profiteth me
    nothing.

Charity suffereth long, and is kind; charity envieth not; charity
    vaunteth not itself, is not puffed up,

Doth not behave itself unseemly, seeketh not her own, is not easily
    provoked, thinketh no evil;

Rejoiceth not in iniquity, but rejoiceth in the truth;

Beareth all things, believeth all things, hopeth all things, endureth all
    things.

Charity never faileth: but whether there be prophecies, they shall fail;
    whether there be tongues, they shall cease; whether there be
    knowledge, it shall vanish away.

For we know in part, and we prophesy in part.

But when that which is perfect is come, then that which is in part shall
    be done away.

When I was a child, I spake as a child, I understood as a child, I thought as a child: but when I became a man, I put away childish things.

For now we see through a glass, darkly; but then face to face: now I know in part; but then shall I know even as also I am known.

And now abideth faith, hope, charity, these three; but the greatest of these is charity.

The Bible, King James Version

The Truly Great

I think continually of those who were truly great,
Who, from the womb, remembered the soul's history
Through corridors of light, where the hours are sun,
Endless and singing. Whose lovely ambition
Was that their lips, still touched with fire,
Should tell of the Spirit, clothed from head to foot in song.
And who hoarded from the Spring branches
The desires falling across their bodies like blossoms.

What is precious, is never to forget
The essential delight of the blood drawn from ageless springs
Breaking through rocks in worlds before our earth.
Never to deny its pleasure in the morning simple light
Nor its grave evening demand for love.
Never to allow gradually the traffic to smother
With noise and fog, the flowering of the Spirit.

Near the snow, near the sun, in the highest fields,
See how these names are fèted by the waving grass
And by the streamers of white cloud
And whispers of wind in the listening sky.
The names of those who in their lives fought for life,
Who wore at their hearts the fire's centre.
Born of the sun, they travelled a short while toward the sun
And left the vivid air signed with their honour.

Stephen Spender

The Summer Day

Who made the world?
Who made the swan, and the black bear?
Who made the grasshopper?
This grasshopper, I mean—
the one who has flung herself out of the grass,
the one who is eating sugar out of my hand,
who is moving her jaws back and forth instead of up and down—
who is gazing around with her enormous and complicated eyes.
Now she lifts her pale forearms and thoroughly washes her face.
Now she snaps her wings open, and floats away.
I don't know exactly what a prayer is.
I do know how to pay attention, how to fall down
into the grass, how to kneel down in the grass,
how to be idle and blessed, how to stroll through the fields,
which is what I have been doing all day.
Tell me, what else should I have done?
Doesn't everything die at last, and too soon?
Tell me, what is it you plan to do
with your one wild and precious life?

Mary Oliver

The Human Seasons

Four Seasons fill the measure of the year;
　There are four seasons in the mind of man:
He has his lusty Spring, when fancy clear
　Takes in all beauty with an easy span:
He has his Summer, when luxuriously
　Spring's honey'd cud of youthful thought he loves
To ruminate, and by such dreaming high
　Is nearest unto heaven: quiet coves
His soul has in its Autumn, when his wings
　He furleth close; contented so to look
On mists in idleness—to let fair things
　Pass by unheeded as a threshhold brook.
He has his Winter too of pale misfeature,
Or else he would forego his mortal nature.

John Keats

My Life Has Been the Poem

My life has been the poem I would have writ,
But I could not both live and utter it.

Henry David Thoreau

A Final Affection

I love the accomplishments of trees,
How they try to restrain great storms
And pacify the very worms that eat them.
Even their deaths seem to be considered.

I fear for trees, loving them so much.
I am nervous about each scar on bark,
Each leaf that browns. I want to
Lie in their crotches and sigh,
Whisper of sun and rains to come.

Sometimes on summer evenings I step
Out of my house to look at trees
Propping darkness up to the silence.

When I die I want to slant up
Through those trunks so slowly
I will see each rib of bark, each whorl;
Up through the canopy, the subtle veins
And lobes touching me with final affection;
Then to hover above and look down
One last time on the rich upliftings,
The circle that loves the sun and moon,
To see at last what held the darkness up.

                              Paul Zimmer

Ithaka

When you set out for Ithaka
ask that your way be long,
full of adventure, full of instruction.
The Laistrygonians and the Cyclops,
angry Poseidon—do not fear them:
such as these you will never find
as long as your thought is lofty, as long as a rare
emotion touch your spirit and your body.
The Laistrygonians and the Cyclops,
angry Poseidon—you will not meet them
unless you carry them in your soul,
unless your soul raise them up before you.

Ask that your way be long.
At many a summer dawn to enter
—with what gratitude, what joy—
ports seen for the first time;
to stop at Phoenician trading centres,
and to buy good merchandise,
mother of pearl and coral, amber and ebony,
and sensuous perfumes of every kind,
sensuous perfumes as lavishly as you can;
to visit many Egyptian cities,
to gather stores of knowledge from the learned.
Have Ithaka always in your mind.
Your arrival there is what you are destined for.
But do not in the least hurry the journey.
Better it last for years,
so that when you reach the island you are old,
rich with all you have gained on the way,
not expecting Ithaka to give you wealth.

Ithaka gave you a splendid journey.
Without her you would not have set out.
She hasn't anything else to give you.

And if you find her poor, Ithaka hasn't deceived you.
So wise you have become, of such experience,
that already you will have understood what these Ithakas mean.

Constantine P. Cavafy

Translated from the Modern Greek
by Edmund Keeley and Philip Sherrard

Little Gidding,
The Four Quartets
(excerpt)

We shall not cease from exploration
And the end of all our exploring
Will be to arrive where we started
And know the place for the first time.
Through the unknown, remembered gate
When the last of earth left to discover
Is that which was the beginning;
At the source of the longest river
The voice of the hidden waterfall
And the children in the apple-tree
Not known, because not looked for
But heard, half-heard, in the stillness
Between two waves of the sea.

T. S. Eliot

I Dwell in Possibility

I dwell in Possibility—
A fairer House than Prose—
More numerous of Windows—
Superior—for Doors—

Of Chambers as the Cedars—
Impregnable of Eye—
And for an Everlasting Roof
The Gambrels of the Sky—

Of Visitors—the fairest—
For Occupation—This—
The spreading wide my narrow Hands
To gather Paradise—

Emily Dickinson

(Tuck a Child)

Tuck a child in his bed,
close this letter of life
that will arrive tonight.
We will read it together,
its contents will be spoken
out loud in the dark.

What it contains will end
by creating changes;
we will stop, we will go,
the whole room will capsize
in this sleeping one.

Rainer Maria Rilke
Translated from the
French by A. Poulin, Jr.

THE EDITORS

Susan Todd graduated from Smith College and is the mother of three grown daughters. She was an elementary school teacher for many years before becoming head of the Heath School in Heath, Massachusetts. She was a founding editor of *Parents' Choice* magazine and a contributing editor of *FamilyFun* magazine. Her retrospective on Laura Ingalls Wilder appeared in the *Atlantic Monthly*. Susan lives in Ashfield, Massachusetts.

Carol Purington has been writing haiku and tanka poems since 1980. Her works have appeared in many English-language haiku/tanka publications, both print and online, and they have won recognition in international contests. She has published two books of haiku (*Woodslawn Farm* and *Family Farm*) and three books of tanka (*The Trees Bleed Sweetness, A Pattern for This Place,* and *Gathering Peace*). Carol lives on a multigenerational farm in Colrain, Massachusetts.

ACKNOWLEDGMENTS

Our first debt of gratitude is to the poets whose work inhabits these pages. As we have read and reread each poem, we have rejoiced in the good fortune that their words are now part of our own interior lives. We are blessed that the art of these poets has preserved moments of grace and wisdom.

Certain of these poets have helped us with a generosity both literary and practical, without which this collection would not have been possible. They include Richard Wilbur, Mary Oliver, Mary Jo Salter, Rebecca Okrent, Patti Smith, Thomas Yeomans, Rachel Hadas, Sharon Olds, Joan Baez, Billy Collins, and Susie Patlove.

We also are indebted to many anthologists over the centuries—from Francis Palgrave to Garrison Keillor. Because of their vision we not only delve into the minds of the poets, but the minds of the anthologists as well, whose selections have caused us to see poetry afresh.

A humbling serendipity has informed the choice of more than a few poems in this book. Some poems we have known for many years, but others have come our way through a chance conversation or encounter.

We thank all those who put poems in our path, especially Mariel Kinsey, Daniel Hall, Matthew Glassman, Elizabeth West, Mary Snow, Beth Clements, Carol O'Hare, Walter McDonald, Tamara Adkins, Jeanne Braham, Barbara Maltby, Frances Kidder, and Noy Holland.

Those who helped set our course early on include Jonathan Diamond, Tracy Kidder, Stephen Young, Neil Astley, William Pritchard, Peter Coyote, Dana Gioia, Catherine Newman, and Larry Kimmel. Larry, his wife Kathleen Leahy, Susannah Lee, along with Susie Patlove, were vital during the proofreading stage. We are grateful also to Karyn Rosencranz, Bruce Rabb, Pat Leuchtman, Renée Walbert, Ike Williams, Ann Hallock, Ellen Doré Watson, Don Purington, Rose Marie Morse, Jan Freeman, J. D. McLatchy, Bobbie Kinnell, Larry and Carol Sheehan, and several unnamed angels for the myriad ways they supported this endeavor.

With pleasure and awe we think back to the teachers we had in high school and college who opened the world of poetry to us: Marie Saunders, Robert Nichols, William Sweeney, Walter Bauer, Dorothy Dromeshauser, Sylvan Schendler, and Alfred Dixon.

Many children in our lives intensified and enriched our work on this book. We honor them all, especially Thomas Eamonn Harte, whose arrival was the occasion for the first *Morning Song,* and his brother, James Bishop, who has found his own lilt in language.

We will forever think with gratitude of Mike Steinig, whom we call our First Reader. He wrote that he had never spent much time with poetry, and then described the engagement and delight he felt as he sat with the *Morning Song* manuscript on his lap and read aloud night after night to his wife as she was feeding their infant twin sons before sleep. Rebecca Ascher-Walsh, Rebecca Kramer, Rachel Godlewski, Ruth Craft, Rebecca Jacobson, Mary Bagg, Maureen Shea, and Chris Stockman gave insightful early readings.

Our agent Betsy Lerner scaled the publishing mountain carrying a book of poetry with courage and faith and continues to provide invaluable counsel and kindness. We are indebted to our first editor at St. Martin's Press, Lindsay Sagnette, who from the start understood and loved this collection. We thank George Witte for his magnanimous shepherding of Morning Song to completion, a quality that surely emanates from his own sensitivities as a poet. We couldn't have hoped for a more experienced and assiduous copy editor than David Stanford Burr. Also at St. Martin's we are grateful to Jaime Ariza, John Karle, Jeanne-Marie Hudson, Nicole Lawson, Loren Jaggers, Kathryn Parise, and Steve Snider for giving such thought and energy to Morning Song. We thank Terra Layton for all her careful assistance with coordination. Fred Courtright of The Permissions Company, with his tireless sang froid, was absolutely essential in helping us acquire the permissions.

The joy felt by our families in Morning Song has only increased our own. For their enduring enthusiasm and depth of knowledge, Emily and Liam, Maisie and James, and Nell and Mike touch the heart. Maisie's drawings, so full of life and wit, are a priceless gift. Again and again Robert Bagg led us by the hand, opened doors, walked us through, and never let us doubt the worth of this book. He was indispensable.

Stephanie Purington, our steadfast and creative partner since the days when she made the original gift volume, has perseveringly offered strength, reassurance, and mathematical realism. Her daughters, Katy and Elizabeth, offered great curatorial assistance. Barbara Purington's remarkable involvement, always attentive and good humored, has sustained us through every step and in every detail. Herbert Purington, a man of few words, said from the beginning, "I think you have something."

For Richard Todd's erudition and expertise, whether about commas or contracts or poetic conceptions or just getting the manuscript out the door, we feel gratitude far beyond what words can express. Every sentence of encouragement or advice he offered contained music and merriment. Whenever there was a dilemma to be solved, he was at hand, and thus he became our beloved Editor of Last Resort.

COPYRIGHT
ACKNOWLEDGMENTS